D0518550

ONE HUNDRED AND ONE THINGS FOR THE HOUSEWIFE TO DO

1949

PLATE I FRONTISPIECE

FURNISHING FABRICS SHOULD BE SELECTED
WITH DUE REGARD TO COLOUR & PATTERN.

Foreword by the Publisher

Britain in 1949 was still in the grips of rationing from
World War II and the make-do-and-mend ethos is more than
evident in the faithful reproduction of this 1949 publication.

101 Things for the Housewife to Do was one of the many books that
Batsford published in the first half of the 20th century. It was
part of the long-running and much-loved *101 Things* series,
which started in the 1920s and included *101 Things for Little Folk
to Do, 101 Things for a Boy to Make, 101 Games to Make and Play* and
101 Things to Do in Wartime. The authors of many of the books in
the series, Lillie B. Horth and husband Arthur C. Horth, between
them, helped foster the British crafting tradition. Whether the
housewife was after advice on household chores, useful hobbies
for themselves and wholesome ones for their children, the
Horths had the answers.

The vast majority of the 101 suggestions are a wonderful mixture
of lady-like preoccupations ('Cleaning Gloves' and 'Hat
Wardrobe') and no-nonsense sensible advice for the home, such
as 'Fixing Loose Knife Handles' and 'Hobbies for the Children'.
In today's world of instant gratification, concern about nutrition
and children's behaviour, there is so much that is refreshing in
this book and so much that is as relevant now as it was nearly 60
years ago. The book is a wonderful insight into the changing
roles of women and family life generally after the war, but more
than anything else, its many old-fashioned household tips are as
useful as ever.

Tina Persaud, Publisher
B T Batsford 2007

101 THINGS FOR THE HOUSEWIFE TO DO
1949

A PRACTICAL HANDBOOK
FOR THE HOME

BY

LILLIE B. & ARTHUR C. HORTH

B. T. BATSFORD, LTD.

LONDON · NEW YORK · TORONTO · SYDNEY

First published 1939
Second Edition 1949
Reprinted 2007

By B T Batsford
The Old Magistrates Court
10 Southcombe Street
London W14 0RA

An imprint of Anova Books Company Ltd

ISBN 9780713490565

A CIP catalogue record for this book is available from the British Library.

15 14 13 12 10 09 08 07
10 9 8 7 6 5 4 3 2

Printed by SNP Leefung Printers Ltd, China

This book can be ordered direct from the publisher at the website:
www.anovabooks.com, or try your local bookshop.

AUTHORS' PREFACE

In response to innumerable requests the authors have written this book to accompany the previous volumes of the " 101 Series," which have in turn catered for Boys, Girls, Little Folks and the Handyman. The success of the series leads the authors to hope that their efforts to help the Housewife will meet with approval.

The wide scope of household duties makes it difficult to cover every aspect of the Housewife's work, but as far as possible within the limits of 213 pages, a considerable amount of information has been included. The necessity for recreation and physical culture has not been overlooked, and suggestions are given for suitable occupations for children.

One branch of the Housewife's duties, that of cooking, has not been treated in detail ; there are, however, so many cookery books which deal fully with the subject, that it has not been thought necessary to supplement them. It is hoped that the section dealing with First Aid Remedies and the illustrated instructions on Bandaging will be of great help.

The authors wish to acknowledge with gratitude much valuable help from a large circle of friends, too numerous to mention, who by helpful suggestions and criticism have made the book more useful, and they would like to thank all those who have so kindly lent illustrations and provided practical information.

Special thanks are due to Messrs. Morton Sundour Fabrics, Ltd., for the Colour Plates, to Messrs. Thomas French & Co., Ltd., proprietors of " Rufflette " brand tape and curtain fitments for much valuable information, and the illustrations on pages 10, 11, 17, 19, 23, 24, 27 and 29; to Dryad Handicrafts for photographs and diagrams on pages 46, 49, 164, 173, 174 and 177; to Messrs. Heal & Sons for the illustrations of furniture appearing on pages 7, 8, 13 and 14; to Messrs. Weldons, Ltd., and Messrs. Geo. Newnes for permission to reproduce illustrations by the authors which have appeared in their publications; to the Women's League of Health and Beauty for the illustrated section dealing with Physical Culture, as well as to the proprietors of " Brillo," the Chiswick Products, Ltd., proprietors of " Varnene," the Electrolux Co., Harbutts Plasticine, the Hurley Machine Co., manufacturers of the Thor Stowaway Kitchen Laundry, Hoovers Ltd., Liberty and Co., Ltd., and Mrs. Roberts for lending the specimen of Needle Weaving.

L. B. AND A. C. HORTH.

GUILDFORD.

CONTENTS

		PAGE
PREFACE	v
Planning Household Duties	1
Arranging the Menus	2
Colour Schemes	4
Selecting Furniture	6
Bedroom Furnishing	9
Furnishing the Day Nursery	12
Furnishing for Comfort and Decoration . . .	15
Period Designs in Furnishing	16
Making Loose Covers	20
Fabrics for the Home	22
Fitting Curtain Hooks and Rails	26
Curtains and Valances	28
Needle Weaving	31
Decorative Stitches	32
Washing and Ironing by Electricity . . .	34
Carpet Sweeping	37
Pelmet Styles	38
Supports for Pelmets	40
Making Lampshades	42
Everlasting Flower Decoration	44
Seating with Sea-Grass	47
Reseating in Cane	50
Hobbies for Housewives	52
The Care of Household Brushes	53
Miniature Table Gardens	54
Bulbs in Bowls	57
A Bulb Basket	58
Window Gardening	60
Extra Shelves in the Pantry	62

CONTENTS

	PAGE
Care of Refrigerators	64
Fitting Kitchen Shelves	67
Easily made Window Seat	68
Making a Modern Divan Bed	70
Fitting a New Washer	72
Mending Electric Cords or Flex	74
Renewing a Burnt-out Fuse	76
Reading the Meters	78
Using Thermometers	80
Weights and Measures	82
Hat Wardrobe	84
Shoe Tidy	84
Making Wastepaper Baskets	86
Upholstered Boxes	88
Care of the Sewing Machine	90
Using Sewing Machine Attachments	93
Making Cushions	94
How to make Pouffes	96
Marking Linen	98
Darning Table Linen and Towels	100
Cleaning Pots and Pans	103
Mending Pots and Pans	104
Repairing Broken Crockery	106
Fixing Tiles and Repairing Fireplaces	108
Furniture Polishes and Revivers	111
Keeping Scissors and Knives in good trim	112
Fixing Loose Knife Handles	114
When the Sink is stopped up	116
Removing Stains	118
Preparing Floors for Staining	120
Staining and Polishing Floors	122
Cleaning and Repairing Wallpaper	125
Cleaning Distempered Walls	126
Cleaning Paint Work	128
Easing Doors and Drawers	130
Re-polishing with Shellac	132

CONTENTS

	PAGE
Using Paint and Enamel	134
Matching and Patching Linoleum	136
Repairing and Binding Carpets	138
Keeping the Gas Stove in Good Condition . .	140
Electric Irons and Ironing	143
Cleaning Carpets	144
Removing Marks on Polished Surfaces . . .	145
Washing Fabrics	146
Simple Dry Cleaning	149
Cleaning Gloves	150
Dealing with the Moth Pest	152
Trays and Partitions for Drawers	154
Exterminating Mice	156
Household Pests	158
Storing Fabrics	159
Building Dolls' Houses	160
Modelling for the Children	162
Hobbies for Children	165
Doll's Furniture in Paper	166
Toys from Match-Boxes	168
First Aid Cupboard	170
Weaving	172
Looms for Weaving	176
Simple Home Dyeing	178
Decorative Dyeing	182
Physical Culture	185
Care of the Teeth, Hands and Feet	191
Care of the Complexion and Hair	192
First Aid Remedies	195
First Aid Bandaging	206
Using Roller Bandages	208
Ankle, Arm and Knee Bandages	210
Methods of Stopping Bleeding	212
INDEX	214

PLANNING HOUSEHOLD DUTIES

The control of a home requires method if it is to be carried out with any degree of success. Just as much care and attention is needed in the provision of food and the supervision of a few rooms as in a large mansion.

The two main items to be considered are money and time. One controls the extent of the house, the amount of equipment and the cost of living, the other is of equal importance because on proper arrangement of time, the smooth running of the home depends.

The financial side of the housewife's duties should be conducted on business lines. The total expenditure should be planned to cover all ordinary possibilities As a rule, the budget should be arranged to provide for regular yearly, quarterly, monthly and weekly expenses.

These expenses will include such working costs as rent, wages, fuel and light, cleaning materials, stores, telephone and various sundries. The amount available for the purchase and upkeep of the wardrobe should be determined, and the expenses relating to the upkeep of the house such as rates and taxes, insurances, garden and upkeep. A special account for food should be kept and there should be an account to cover such items as education, doctor and medicine, holidays, subscriptions, newspapers and library and postal expenses. Finally, the housewife should be able to allocate a proportion of the income as purely personal expenditure to include clothing, toilet necessities and luxuries.

The order and sequence of the daily work is a matter of individual planning, but any time-table should allow of one day, unalloted to any special work in order to allow for emergencies. First arrange for the most important daily tasks, those which must be done. Next the weekly jobs, such as turning out rooms, laundering, leaving some time available for occasional jobs such as checking the household linen and anything else leading to orderly arrangement.

I

ARRANGING THE MENUS

Catering for even a small household calls for careful planning both as to purchase and variety. Apart from the necessity of keeping up the household supplies for the general cleaning, etc., it is necessary to keep a small store of dry and canned goods for use either in emergencies or when perishable foodstuffs are scarce.

Household work can be eased by suitable arrangements of the daily menus throughout the week. It should not be necessary to cook hot meals every day, for, with a little careful planning, appetizing meals can be cooked on one day to cover the meals of two days.

It is not the purpose of this book to deal with the actual processes of cooking or to give particulars of recipes for various dishes, there are innumerable cookery books available, but to give suggestions for the general easing of work in the house. As the provisions of meals is an important item in the daily work, the housewife should be conversant with a wide range of recipes, and be able to arrange for suitable menus.

Cooking in itself is apt to become monotonous, but in a large way this can be avoided by aiming at variety, by doing the old things in a new way ; by devoting some attention to the values of the various foodstuffs, and the need for supplying a well-balanced diet.

Mention has been made several times in these pages of a well-balanced diet, and to attain this desirable achievement a knowledge of the uses of various foods and their effect on health should be understood. Help can be obtained from the Health departments of governments and municipalities and also from many books, but the use of common sense goes a long way.

One of the most important items in the dietary is that of fresh vegetables and fruit. When these foods are at their cheapest they should be used liberally, and it is a good plan, in arranging the budget, to spend any spare money on fresh green vegetables, tomatoes, fruits in season and especially oranges. As a general rule, this kind of food should form at least half of the diet each day, it is essential equally for the growing child and for the adult.

Correct cooking of green vegetables is of considerable importance. The all too prevalent method of boiling such green stuff as cabbages, root crops and potatoes is to be deprecated. Without exception, all vegetables should be steamed, but if they are boiled the water should be used for soup and not thrown away, as it contains valuable salts which are of the utmost value to the health.

Steaming and stewing are economical ways of cooking meat as well, but if meat is to be roasted or baked it is better to do the baking in ovenware, so that all the juices and gravy is retained. Several kinds of pressure cookers are available in which the whole of the meal can be cooked by steam with a minimum of heat. When several meals have to be provided much time can be saved by the use of a pressure cooker, and, in addition, all the food is cooked under ideal conditions.

As far as possible fresh salads should be provided at every meal and if salads are not available, fresh fruit should be substituted. Instead of serving the salad and fruit during or at the end of a meal, it is much more healthful to begin with it. With the fresh salad add a little coarsely grated uncooked root vegetables, carrots, parsnips, turnips, etc. During the summer particularly, sliced apples, pears and other hard fruit can be mixed with the green salad, and as a dressing lemon juice and salad oil is just as palatable and far more beneficial than prepared dressing.

COLOUR SCHEMES

The most successful colour schemes depend not on the colours used but mainly on the proportions in which they are used. The walls and the floor occupy the greater proportion, and as a rule these should be restful. Suitable contrasts can be obtained by the furniture and curtains, cushions, and various small articles.

Individual reaction to colour is so varied that no scheme, however pleasing, will suit all tastes. Some people are able to live with violent contrasts, others find pleasure in harmonising tones. Generally it is safe to begin with a neutral background, that is keep the walls and carpet free from strong colours.

The colour scheme of a room should bear considerable relation to its position. Rooms facing north and having little if any sun should be brighter in tone and colour than those facing south. Strong colours are stimulating and soft tints and shades are restful. As a rule bedrooms should be kept as restful as possible, but living rooms can be brighter and in many cases brilliant.

Many people have favourite colours which they would like to incorporate in the colour scheme, but if the colour should be one of the brilliant primaries such as violet, green, yellow, orange or red, considerable care will be needed to obtain the correct proportion otherwise the value will be lost.

An important point in deciding on colour schemes, and one that is rarely given full consideration, is that of artificial light. Usually the main living room is used more at night than during the day, and many colours which are admirable in sunlight look drab by artificial light.

The numbers on the diagrams on the next page refer to the walls (1), the floor (2), the curtains (3), upholstered furniture, such as armchairs and settees (4), and the small splashes of contrasting colours in such things as cushions, ornaments, and other small useful and decorative fitments (5).

4

ORANGE 5	RED	BLACK
GREEN 4	GREEN	BROWN
YELLOW 3	LIGHT BROWN	PALE PINK
BROWN 2	DARK BROWN	BLUE GREY
GREY 1	FAWN.	NEUTRAL GREY

YELLOW	PALE GREEN	RED
GREY	GREY	GREEN
ORANGE	FAWN	WHITE
BLUE	GREEN	BROWN
CREAM	PALE ORANGE	YELLOW

GREEN	PALE MAUVE	MAUVE
MAUVE	DARK MAUVE	DARK BLUE
PALE BLUE	PALE BLUE	WHITE
BROWN	DARK BLUE	OCHRE
PALE BLUE	GREY	PALE PINK

SELECTING FURNITURE

In the selection of furniture for modern homes, consideration must be given to fitness for purpose. The tendency is towards small rooms and, especially in flats, economy of space is an important matter. Useful double purpose furniture is convenient, as for example the combined sideboard and dining table and the bookcase reading chair. Ornate decoration has given way to simplicity and ostentatiousness to comfort. The housewife in the choice of furniture looks to the saving of labour, and therefore highly carved and moulded cabinetwork has little attraction.

Three typical examples of modern furniture are shown on the next page. The top photograph shows a setting for the corner of a lounge or for a man's study. The bookcases are made of a number of units of various sizes. Additions can be made to accommodate a growing library. The secretaire or writing-desk has bookshelves at its side. The easy chair, plainly upholstered, has side pieces which rest the head.

The centre photograph is a suggestion for a diningroom for a small house or cottage. The furniture is waxed oak, it is easily cleaned and there are no inaccessible dust traps. The standard lamp is in keeping with the general scheme. The small dining table is designed to occupy a small space, the stools fit underneath when the table is not in use. The dresser sideboard is an attractive piece of plain furniture, and besides being useful is highly decorative.

The bottom photograph shows a different setting for a study or the corner of a lounge. The furniture is in weathered oak. The bookcases are made with flat sides, they can be butted together or used separately. The armchair has flat topped arms, useful for a book, ashtray or glass. There is a folding flap on one side to form a table and space for books on the other side.

A SETTING
FOR THE
CORNER
OF A
LOUNGE OR
A STUDY.

SUITABLE
FURNITURE
FOR A SMALL
DINING
ROOM.

ANOTHER
SETTING
FOR A
LOUNGE OR
STUDY.

Photographs by Heal & Sons.

7

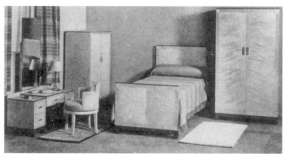

*Three Photographs of Modern Bedroom Furniture
by Heal & Sons.*

8

BEDROOM FURNISHING

Simplicity combined with soft colour harmonies is the keynote of modern bedroom furnishings. Ornate bedsteads, elaborately panelled wardrobes and dressing tables have given way to those with plain surfaces and pleasing proportions.

The ideal bedroom should have patternless walls, either plain paper covered or distempered, the ceiling should tone with the walls, the floor should be either plain boards, stained and polished or covered with plywood panels, plain linoleum or rubber and furnished with soft rugs. If a carpet is desired, it should be a soft short pile, mainly plain with a toned border.

Bedsteads should have solid heads and feet and rely on the decorative quality of the wood for effect. Wardrobes and dressing tables should have plain surfaces so that they can be kept free from dust with the least possible trouble. Superfluous furniture should be avoided in a bedroom. Extra wardrobe room can be provided by a large box under the bed, but it should be provided with easy running castors for quick removal.

The top illustration on page 8 shows a curl sycamore bedroom suite. All the pieces illustrated are bow fronted with flutings at the corners. The photograph immediately below shows an inexpensive sycamore suite with walnut bases and margins. In both cases the floors are covered with plain carpets with rugs to give a contrast.

Care should be taken in furnishing bedrooms for children who are beyond the nursery stage. In addition to a small wardrobe for clothes, provision should be made for study. The floor of children's bedrooms should be carpetless as a rule, but two or three soft rugs should be provided. A plain linoleum or rubber will be found more satisfactory than polished boards as they are more easily cleaned. In view of the necessity for cleanliness, only essential furniture should be used.

STEP 1.—Sew " Rufflette " Tape at top and bottom, over the hem at the top of curtain.

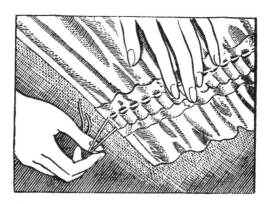

STEP 2.—With curtain lying flat, knot cords at *one* end and pleat by pulling from other end.

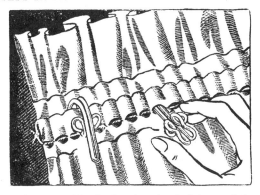

STEP 3.—Slip hooks (or rings) into pockets, turnover fashion. No stitching is necessary. Use rings for rod, hooks for runner rail.

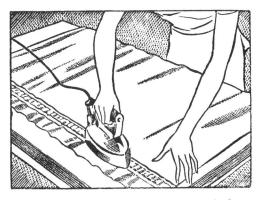

WASHING.—Slip out hooks or rings, untie draw-cords and pull curtain flat. Wash and iron. Then re-pleat and insert hooks as before.

FURNISHING THE DAY NURSERY

In selecting a room for a day nursery or play room for the small children, either a south, south-east or south-west aspect should be chosen. The furniture should be simple with, as far as possible, rounded edges. As it is essential that a nursery should at all times be kept scrupulously clean, considerable attention should be paid to suitable floor coverings ; either linoleum or rubber makes an ideal covering, but both large and small rugs can be used ; ordinary carpets not easily removable for cleaning should be avoided.

Although white enamelled furniture is comparatively inexpensive, it is not entirely satisfactory in wear, plain oak, beech and birch are to be preferred, and when wax-polished are easily kept clean.

Lighting and heating are important items for the nursery. The windows should be large and should allow free access to the rays of the sun. In fine weather it should be possible to open the window to allow of plenty of fresh air. Central heating is the ideal for the nursery, but where it cannot be arranged, it is better to use an electric radiator or a gas stove rather than an open fire, and protection provided by a strong metal guard. Modern electric heating fitments can be attached to the walls well above the reach of children and are an effective method of heating.

Decoration in the nursery can take the form of friezes. The walls should be distempered in a luminous colour ; white walls are not advisable. The lower portion of the wall can be painted with a suitable enamel so that finger marks can be easily washed off.

A profusion of toys should be avoided. In any case, provision should be made for the storage of the greater proportion of the toys in every day use, either large boxes or cupboards being used. As the children grow up they should be encouraged to make their own toys and find their own amusement.

SUGGESTIONS FOR NURSERY FURNITURE BY
HEAL & SONS.

13

A PLEASING CORNER FURNISHED BY HEAL & SONS.

The settee is kidney shaped with a fluted back, spring stuffed seat and a loose cushion filled with feather and down. The circular coffee table is made in birch, the floor standard lamp is of waxed oak with a fluted buckram shade. The rug is a Donegal hand tufted.

FURNISHING FOR COMFORT AND DECORATION

The choosing of new furniture, the selection of wall coverings, curtains and floor coverings should not be undertaken in any haphazard manner ; a definite scheme should be thought out very carefully so that comfort and decoration enter into it.

Fortunately there is no such thing as a general standard of good taste, and there is scope for individual effort in arranging the contents of the house to give pleasure in its appearance. Colour schemes and modernity can be carried to excess, the aim should be real fitness for the purpose.

There are many articles of furniture, although not intended to form a suite, which may be grouped together in a room without appearing incongruous, but, as a rule, there should be some connecting link to bind the contents of the room into one harmonious whole. The colouring of the walls and the carpet, for example, may tone ; the curtains and the cushions can be made of fabrics similar in colourings and providing a contrast.

In planning a room first make a list of the essential furniture, including nothing more than is necessary. The main pieces of furniture for a dining or bedroom should be made of the same kind of wood. In a lounge this is not necessary as the bigger chairs and settee should be upholstered, but it is not essential that all the upholstery should be carried out in the same fabric, although clashes in colour and pattern should be avoided.

The selection of new furniture depends mainly on the depth of the purse, but well-made and comfortable pieces can be purchased at reasonable prices. When it can be afforded, the best quality is generally the cheapest in the end. A few really good pieces of furniture, selected for comfort and beauty, give a room a far more pleasing appearance than one having an excess.

PERIOD DESIGNS IN FURNISHING

The furniture of various periods is well defined, and in many houses there are examples of old furniture which have either family associations or special attractions of their own. It is often difficult to fit in old pieces of furniture with modern conditions, but fabrics may be made to play an important part in blending furniture of modern design with that of past periods.

As a general guide to the main historical periods of furnishing, the following notes with illustrations of typical fabrics will be helpful.

TUDOR or ELIZABETHAN. During this period the family mansion took the place of the feudal castle. Conditions of life became safer, and the classes below the nobility built and furnished houses. Oak panelling, substantial furniture and various fabrics, including carpets, were introduced. Tapestry was prominent.

JACOBEAN. During this period, walnut with twist turning began to replace oak for chairs, tables and cabinets, and the famous tapestries of Brussels, Gobelin, Aubusson, and Beauvais were imitated. The influence of the Roundheads tended towards simplicity, and upholstery in leather replaced for a time the more luxurious designs of the Louis XIV and the Italian baroque periods.

QUEEN ANNE. Walnut furniture became predominant during the periods from 1680. Embroidery became fashionable for the newly-produced loose upholstered seats of chairs and stools, the usual design being a centre of flowers, or figures framed in trailing flowers and leaves. Curtains in pairs appeared as a decorative feature to match the bed draperies, and pelmets and valances became general. Wood carving together with elaborate inlaying, lacquer and gilt formed the main characteristics of cabinet work.

GEORGIAN. This period showed a great advance in furniture design due to the influence of Thomas

ELIZABETHAN

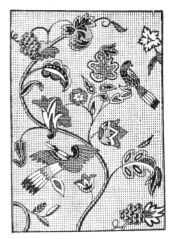

JACOBEAN

WILLIAM & MARY

GEORGIAN

Chippendale. Decoration took on a lighter touch and greater refinement. This period also saw a great development in weaving and silk fabrics which were produced in beautiful designs. Block printing began to replace the old resist dyeing, and still remains as an admirable method of decorating in pattern. Other introductions during this period were wallpaper and lace curtains.

REGENCY. Named from the Prince Regent who became George IV, this period saw continued advances in furniture and fabric design; it was the age of Adam, Sheraton and Hepplewhite, who did more than any other designers to fashion taste. New timbers were used by the cabinet maker, satinwood being popular.

Mechanical inventions were the direct means of enormously increased consumption of furnishing fabrics owing to the lower prices at which they could be obtained. The invention of roller printing resulted in a vast output of printed cottons and chintzes.

VICTORIAN. This period witnessed a great development of mechanical processes but also a great decline in taste. Increasing demands were made by the middle classes owing to the enormous development in the industrial areas and the increasing wealth of the people. Improvements in furnishing were mainly technical and rarely artistic. One great name stands out, that of William Morris, who, in the midst of a riot of machine-made designs reproduced with little or no regard to appropriateness, strove to bring back public taste to naturalness and simplicity.

MODERN. With the return of sanity in design and its influence on machine-made goods, much of the deplorable furniture and furnishings of Victorian days is disappearing, and suitability for purpose has more effect than florid decoration. Furniture is being designed for comfort and use first; the need for utilising space in small houses and flats, and the demand for inexpensive yet pleasing fabrics, has had a great influence in production.

REGENCY

VICTORIAN

EDWARDIAN

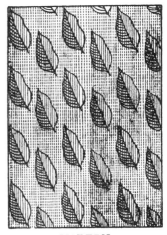

MODERN

19

MAKING LOOSE COVERS

Loose covers should not be considered merely as a protection for delicate and expensive fabrics or a means of hiding worn or faded upholstery, but as one way of altering the appearance of a room. For example, a set of loose covers in warm and stimulating colours can be used during the dark winter days on chairs upholstered in light tones more suitable for the summer. Alternatively, rooms can be toned down and entirely changed by judicious alterations in the colouring of the curtains.

There are a number of materials which are suitable for loose covers, these include cretonnes, printed linens, and glazed and semi-glazed chintzes. Plain materials such as casement cloth and repps are useful as contrasts to patterned carpets and walls. In every case the material used for loose covers should be strong, and unless plain fabrics are of good quality they will show creases.

Considerable care is needed when measuring up for loose covers ; they should be a good fit, but allowance must be made in the case of washable fabrics. Some fabrics shrink more than others, and the possible amount of shrinkage should be ascertained before the material is made up.

Loose covers for chairs and settees are usually made with " tuckaways " down the sides and back of the seat to help the cover to keep in position. The visible seams and joins are best finished with piping ; this may be done with the same material or with a contrast, or in the case of a figured fabric, with a plain colour to tone.

About 9 in. should be added to measurements for tuckaways on the inside back, the seat and the inside arms. If a frill is used, take the total measurement of the chair all round and add 50 per cent. for fullness. Rufflette curtain pocket tape should be sewn at the bottom edge of the frill so that it can be pulled up as tight as the top. This is a simple method of keeping the cover neat and tidy at the bottom of the chair.

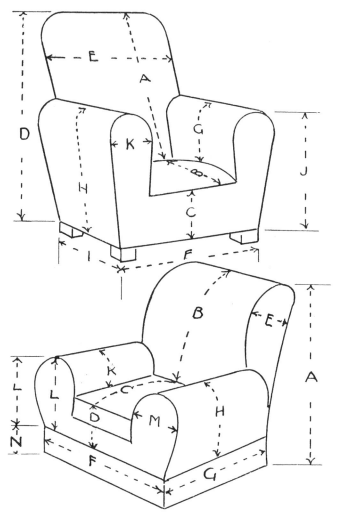

METHODS OF MEASURING AN EASY CHAIR FOR A
LOOSE COVER.

FABRICS FOR THE HOME

Colour, texture and pattern are the important qualities to be considered in the selection of suitable fabrics for use in the home as well as for personal clothing. The greater proportion of fabrics in ordinary use are manufactured by machinery and are produced in great quantities and it is often difficult to make a selection.

The most successful fabrics are those in which the yarns, weave, design, colour and finish are harmoniously combined to produce a fabric suitable in all respects for its purpose. In particular, the closeness of the weave must be in keeping with the object to be served.

Cotton fibres consist of the hairs which are attached to the seed pods of the cotton plant and cotton is one of the cheapest fabrics. It is manufactured up into a variety of forms ; many fabrics once made of linen are now made of cotton ; these include nainsooks, cambrics, lawns, sheetings and shirtings. Cotton is also blended with wool in the manufacture of many household fabrics.

Linen fabrics are woven from yarns spun from the bast fibres obtained from the flax plant. Linen was probably the first known vegetable textile fibre and mummy cloths of linen are known to be at least 6,000 years old. Apart from the value of linen as one of the most durable of fabrics, and its use for table cloths, dress material, etc., linen fabrics are excellent for use as upholstery and the new finishing processes have rendered them admirable for cushions, curtains, etc.

Wool, like linen, has been used for thousands of years. The quality of the fleeces used in its manufacture vary considerably. Wool is an exceedingly valuable member of the textile family, as it possesses several important qualities that are not equalled by any of the other fibres. Wool is naturally crease-resisting owing to its inherent elasticity. It has the property of absorbing twice as much moisture as cotton without feeling damp.

Silk is unique in that it does not require to be spun

CHINTZ.

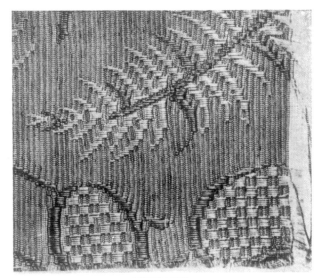

BROCADE.

SATIN DAMASK.

TAPESTRY.

24

like other natural fibres. It is expensive because the crop is very limited compared with other fibres such as cotton, flax and wool. Owing to its properties of absorbing moisture without a feeling of clamminess to the skin and of retaining heat, it is an ideal fabric for wear next the skin.

Rayon is the first machine-made fibre and is made by converting cellulose, obtained from wood pulp, into filaments by a lengthy series of chemical and mechanical processes. The greatest weaknesses of rayon are its loss of strength when wet and its small elasticity. Rayon yarns do not hold dirt as tenaciously as most other fibres, and this is helpful in laundering, but considerable care is required in handling wet fabric.

The principal furnishing fabrics are Bedford Cord, which is characterised by more or less rounded and well defined cords running lengthwise of the fabric. Brocade, formerly used to denote rich silk fabrics, is now applied mainly to ordinary fabrics. Casement cloth is a term covering many lightweight furnishing fabrics. It is most commonly applied to a plain weave texture somewhat heavier than an average quality of plain cotton, but not so tightly woven so that it drapes more gracefully. Fabrics made half-cotton and half-rayon are becoming popular as casement cloths. Chintz is a glazed cotton cloth and is a poor material to use if it is necessary to wash it. Corduroy is a strong cloth with a weft pile surface. The weft is usually cotton, but in the best qualities is of wool. It is woven grey and piece dyed. Crash is a strong, coarse linen fabric made with inferior flax. Cretonne is a general term applied to an extensive range of cotton fabrics. Damasks are produced from the finest linen yarns, but are imitated in cotton. Moquette is usually a wool or ramie pile on a cotton ground, it may be plain or figured. Repps are reversible fabrics used for upholstery as well as curtains. Tapestry is now made on the power loom and produced in a variety of patterns.

FITTING CURTAIN HOOKS AND RAILS

To be effective, curtains should run easily and drape gracefully, and this can only be done by using suitable fitments. With the aid of Rufflette brand tape and hooks, as illustrated on the next page, the housewife will have no difficulty in hanging the curtains.

The majority of curtain rail fittings provide for the hand-drawing of curtains along the rail, the suspension between the rail and the curtains being effected by the use of a small runner wheel.

When handling heavy curtains especially, and for all purposes where a cord-controlled curtain rail is required, the Rufflette fittings are ideal, the operation of the cords is simply yet ingeniously designed, and the fittings do not show when the curtains are drawn.

Net curtains are sometimes hung on spring curtain wire, extending rods, wooden rods and brass rails, the latter, when flat is the neatest and most effective. This form of rail, also called the glass rail, can be used with and without gliders as indicated on the next page. By sewing Rufflette $\frac{1}{2}$ in. tape to the curtain heading, and looping the special pockets of the tape on to special gliders, the curtains can be moved to and fro at will, and at the same time keep their shape perfect and draping even.

When measuring for curtain rails which are to overlap in the centre, allow 6 in. more than the window measurement and, where possible, 3 in. on each side beyond the window frame. For windows in a recess it is a good thing to have the curtains clear of the window sill. It is advisable to wipe curtain rails regularly with an oily rag, damp atmosphere is liable to corrode the metal. If the curtain rail cannot be fixed direct to the wood-work of the window frame, it is usual to provide a suitable strip of wood about 2 in. by 1 in. and secure it to the wall with Rawlplugs.

"GLASS" RAIL CURTAIN (NO GLIDERS USED).

THE "RUFFLETTE" R.77 FIX-PLEAT HOOK NOT ONLY SUPPORTS BUT HOLDS THE PLEATS IN THE "RUFFLETTE" CURTAIN POCKET TAPE FIRMLY IN POSITION.

SECTION OF CURTAIN RAIL AND VALANCE USED WHERE CURTAINS ARE HAND DRAWN.

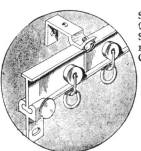

SECTION OF HAND DRAWN CURTAIN RAIL SHOWING SPECIAL BRACKET WHICH BRINGS RAIL CLOSE TO CEILING.

NET CURTAIN RAIL (WITH GLIDERS).

27

CURTAINS AND VALANCES

The popularity of lace net curtains is due to the fact that in day-time they screen the room from the outside without shutting out the light or the view from the room. Good lace curtains are also decorative.

Four typical designs for curtain laces are shown on the opposite page, and these are still in demand for windows of pre-war style. The modern type of casement window usually calls for nets and brise of varying widths, which are either sold by the yard or made in complete units.

Festoon curtains or blinds are in increasing demand, and are particularly suitable for large and also round windows, the festoon blind can be made easily by using Rufflette curtain tape at equal intervals from the top to the bottom of the blind, special curtain rings are inserted in the pocket tape to take the cords.

Simplicity in handling curtains is assured by the use of Rufflette pocket tape ; it is available in widths of $\frac{1}{2}$ in., $\frac{3}{4}$ in., 1 in., $1\frac{1}{4}$ in., and $1\frac{1}{2}$ in. (twin pocket). The $\frac{1}{2}$ in. is used for net size curtains only with a special hook. The pocket is not a hole or a loop, it is actually woven and does not shrink with washing or stretch with wear. The pockets are spaced every $\frac{1}{2}$ in. and ensures evenly-spaced folds without the need for measuring.

Two illustrations showing methods of making valances are shown at the bottom of the previous page. Box pleating is generally effective, but gathered valances look better if given three rows of gauging as indicated. With Rufflette tape, no difficulty will be found in making a valance. The pleats in a box-pleated valance are usually about 2 in. wide and occur every 2 in. or 3 in. along the top ; they are ironed hard down on the heading tape and allowed to open out slightly (but still stiffly) towards the lower edge. For a box-pleated valance, three times the rod measurement should be allowed.

RENAISSANCE.

MARIE ANTOINETTE.

ADAM.

MODERN.

GATHERED VALANCES LOOK
BETTER IF GIVEN THREE
ROWS OF GAUGING.

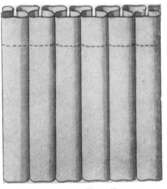

WELL MADE BOX PLEATS
ARE A GOOD FORM OF
SIMPLE VALANCE.

NEEDLE WEAVING ON PLAIN NET.

EFFECTIVE DECORATION OF PLAIN NET CURTAINS.

NEEDLE WEAVING

Needle weaving is one of the most quickly worked and at the same time one of the most effective forms of simple embroidery. Actually it is a method of treating the warp threads when the weft has been withdrawn. Crash, linen, canvas, hessian and net are all suitable.

All kinds of articles can be decorated with needle weaving; the method allows of formal designs to be worked using coloured wools or mercerised cotton. For the purpose of decoration, it is a simple matter to design bright patterns in colour.

In preparing a piece of material for needle weaving in closely woven material the width of the band should be marked out. The width of the pattern is cut between two threads, pull out the top and bottom threads and cut between these two points at the required spot, taking care to cut between the two warp threads. The cut threads are withdrawn after the raw edges of the material have been buttonholed. The threads are now divided into groups by buttonholing or hemstitching.

In weaving, use a blunt needle and a long thread; although not essential it is convenient to use an embroidery frame to keep the threads taut. Simple patterns can be worked by passing the needle backwards and forwards over and under the threads.

Designs for needle weaving can be worked out on squared paper, each square being used to represent a group of threads; it is advisable to plan out patterns containing more than one colour in order to avoid mistakes. It is convenient to work from the centre of a pattern, and care should be taken to press the threads down so that the warp threads are hidden.

The curtain illustrated looks most effective; it is worked in mercerised thread in three colours to tone with the colour scheme of the room. It is just simple needle weaving, worked straight on to the net with a 2 in. hem border and a small pattern either side as shown.

DECORATIVE STITCHES

One of the simplest methods of decoration by stitches is the chain stitch as shown at Fig. 1 at the top of the next page. This stitch is capable of many variations, one of the most useful being the lazy-daisy, and it is used mainly to form small star-like flower shapes. It will be seen that the petals are formed by a long loop held in position by a small stitch as indicated at Fig. 2. When the loops are complete as at Fig. 3, they may be added to and made more decorative as shown at Fig. 4. The above illustrations, from " 101 Things for Girls to Do," are only a few of many devoted to decorative needlework.

Another typical illustration from the same book appears also on the next page and is one accompanying an article on Simple Embroidery Motifs. The flower motif at Fig. 1 is an adaption of the lazy-daisy stitch shown at Fig. 3 above. The motif at Fig. 2 is another adaption of the same stitch. The flower form at Fig. 3 is effective with a back stitch or some other form of line stitch. In the illustration at Fig. 4, the leaves are in back stitch and the stem in crewel stitch. In Fig. 5, the outline of the leaf is in crewel stitch and the veins in back stitch.

Suggestions are given at Figs. 6 and 7, for obtaining an effect of radiation in arranging a pattern. A spray containing leaves can be arranged as indicated at Fig. 6, or the same effect of radiation can be gained by using the spiral. Although it is quite possible to obtain transfers for almost any kind of embroidery work, there is much more satisfaction to be obtained in working out an original pattern, and using creative ability in designing something containing originality of treatment. It is, of course, necessary to have some knowledge of the various stitches which can be used in decorative work in order that effective designs can be worked out.

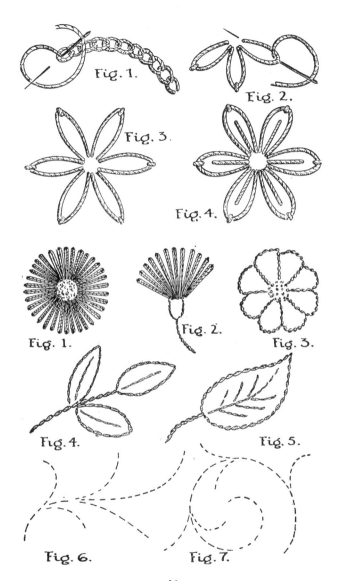

Fig. 1.

Fig. 2.

Fig. 3.

Fig. 4.

Fig. 1.

Fig. 2.

Fig. 3.

Fig. 4.

Fig. 5.

Fig. 6.

Fig. 7.

WASHING AND IRONING BY ELECTRICITY

The kitchen, where the housewife spends a considerable part of the day, can be a model of compactness and yet contain all that is necessary for cooking as well as laundry work. The provision of an electric washing machine means a great saving of time and labour, and in selecting such equipment the inclusion of a mechanical ironer is worth while.

The housewife who is contemplating the addition of a power washer to the kitchen equipment should take into account the ease of operation, the saving of time and energy, and the possibility of doing other things while the machine is at work. But the question of available space for an electric washer is an all important matter in the small kitchens usually to be found in modern houses and flats ; it is, therefore, essential that compactness must be considered.

A new type of electrical aid to washing and ironing is illustrated on the next page and is admirably adapted for use in small kitchens. When not in use it can be lowered by means of the adjustable legs and may be placed under a table, the draining board or in a corner out of the way as it measures only $23\frac{3}{4}$ in. high, $21\frac{5}{8}$ in. wide and $22\frac{1}{2}$ in. deep. It is known as the Thor Stow-a-way Kitchen laundry, and it operates from any wall socket and needs no special plumbing connections.

Although the modern electric washer requires no mechanical attention and usually can be serviced if desired, it does need to be kept clean. After use, the machine should be rinsed in warm water and wiped dry. Being composed of enamelled metal, the work of cleaning is rendered quite easy.

It may happen when hard water is used, that a scum deposit will be left ; this can be removed by a rub with a brush moistened with paraffin, afterwards rinsing with clean warm water and soap. Care should be taken that all water is drained off after use.

WASHING AND IRONING BY THE EASY METHOD.
Photographs of the Thor Stow-a-Way Kitchen Laundry.

CARPET SWEEPING IS EASY WITH A VACUUM CLEANER.
Photograph by Hoover, Ltd.

CARPET SWEEPING

The invention of the carpet sweeper followed by the vacuum cleaner has done away with the drudgery of hand sweeping, and the vacuum cleaner especially does the work most satisfactorily without raising dust. It is now no longer necessary to cover furniture with dust cloths each time the carpet is swept.

The carpet sweeper in the form of a small box on wheels, containing brushes which revolve as the box is pushed along, makes very little dust and quickly removes surface dust; it is not so thorough in its action as the vacuum cleaner, which sucks up the dust.

Vacuum cleaners may be either hand or power driven, the latter being the most satisfactory in general use and should be used if electric current is available. They cost surprisingly little to run and, if serviced from time to time, have a long life.

In selecting a cleaner, it is necessary to take into account the reliability of the manufacturer and the availability of service. A machine that cannot be serviced locally is likely to cause trouble and expense.

Most vacuum cleaners have various attachments such as upholstery brushes, floor brushes, polishers and even sprayers, all efficient and labour saving. Special dusting attachments and appliances are also available.

A vacuum cleaner is not only labour saving and clean in use, but is much more effective in removing the dust from a carpet than the hand brush. The life of a carpet cleaned regularly with a reliable vacuum cleaner is greatly increased and its appearance enhanced.

It is advisable to empty the dust bag each time the cleaner is used. It is not a difficult job to remove the brushes for cleaning, but any necessary oiling or motor attention should be done by the service operator. It should be noted that vacuum cleaners are as useful for cleaning clothes, curtains and drapery as for upholstered furniture.

PELMET STYLES

The pelmet is an English term synonymous with the American and French term "Lambrequin." The modern pelmet is entirely flat and may be made of furnishing buckram or sail cloth. It can be of any shape or design which is in general harmony with the room. In designing a pelmet, an essential point to consider is that of its dimensions in proportion to the height of the room and of the window.

Pelmets are not difficult to make, but they call for accuracy in cutting and neatness in execution. In cutting the material to cover the buckram shape, it is advisable to allow three-quarters of an inch more than the pattern all round and then cut the material to the buckram, turning in the edges and snipping the material where necessary.

The design for the edges of a pelmet requires consideration; there is no fixed rule but it is a good plan to follow the lines of the chair furniture in the room. The materials required to make a pelmet are velour, silk or other curtain material. Furnishing buckram, braid, tassels, motifs and Rufflette curtain pocket tape.

The illustrations on the next page show two quite simple edges at the top; the trimming should follow the lines of the cut-out pattern. The diagonal design is particularly effective in a modern room and allows for contrasts in colour. The same applies in the case of the modern panelled design; in this case there is opportunity for colour harmony. The more ornate design is capable of effective colour treatment.

For a straight window the pelmet should project about 6 in. beyond each side and about 6 in. in front. In the case of a bay window, careful measurements are necessary. A represents the inside length, B the depth, C the length of the main window and D the length of the sides. The pelmet front will be approximately 6 in. in front of these measurements.

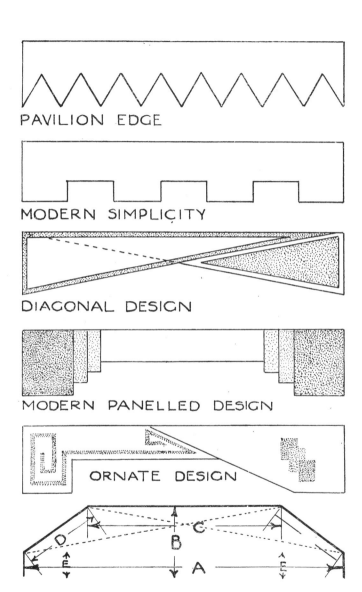

PAVILION EDGE

MODERN SIMPLICITY

DIAGONAL DESIGN

MODERN PANELLED DESIGN

ORNATE DESIGN

39

SUPPORTS FOR PELMETS

Pelmets are fixed to a board or shelf which also carries the curtain rail. Usually the width of the shelf is 6 in., and about 6 in. is allowed for projection beyond the window on each side. The shelf should have a strong support, particularly if heavy curtains are to be used; iron brackets are usual.

The suggestion at the top of the next page shows a pelmet shelf supported by plain angle brackets which are screwed to narrow blocks or strips of wood nailed to the wall on each side of the window frame. In the case of windows with a wide framing, the iron brackets can be attached directly to the framing.

The use of plywood allows for more elaborate shapes to be made; the plywood can be cut to any desired shape and can be screwed to the front and ends of the shelf as indicated on the next page. In the case of square corners, suitable supports should be provided at the corners; these should be cut from wood planed to triangular section and screwed to the shelf.

Pelmet boards with rounded ends are no more difficult to make and fit. A suggestion is given at the bottom of the next page for a curved pelmet of plywood. The entire front, up to the beginning of the curves at the ends should be straight. The curved ends must be screwed to projecting blocks in front, and to the back supports carrying the iron angle brackets. The front blocks should be at least 1 in. square in section. If there should be any difficulty in bending the plywood, make a series of vertical saw-cut at intervals of 1 in. or so down to the first layer of the plywood; these saw-cuts being at the back will not show.

Pelmets for bay windows are made on similar lines, but the shelf must be made up with separate pieces cut to fit the space. The boards should be joined at the top with strips of wood about 2 in. by $\frac{1}{2}$ in. so that the underside is left clear for the curtain rails.

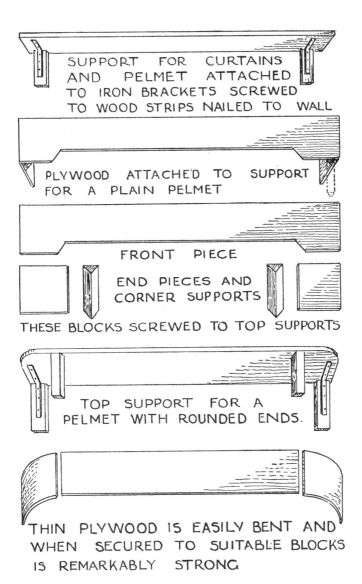

SUPPORT FOR CURTAINS AND PELMET ATTACHED TO IRON BRACKETS SCREWED TO WOOD STRIPS NAILED TO WALL

PLYWOOD ATTACHED TO SUPPORT FOR A PLAIN PELMET

FRONT PIECE

END PIECES AND CORNER SUPPORTS

THESE BLOCKS SCREWED TO TOP SUPPORTS

TOP SUPPORT FOR A PELMET WITH ROUNDED ENDS.

THIN PLYWOOD IS EASILY BENT AND WHEN SECURED TO SUITABLE BLOCKS IS REMARKABLY STRONG

41

MAKING LAMPSHADES

Nowadays lampshades in all shapes and sizes can be inexpensively purchased, but it is not always an easy matter to obtain them in colourings or decorative treatment to suit particular requirements. As the materials for making lampshades are also easily procurable, special shapes and decorative effects can be obtained if they are made at home, not to mention the satisfaction that an original design will provide.

The diagrams on the opposite page show the method of cutting out the shapes for four typical forms of shade. The shapes should be drawn out on squared paper in the first place; the size of the squares will depend on the size of the finished shade, those in the diagrams being based on squares of 1 in.

Many suitable materials are available, the most useful being vellum paper; this is an imitation of real vellum, and is firm enough for use in small shapes without a wire frame. It can be obtained in cream, red, green, pink and orange. Decoration can be carried out with water colour mixed with ox-gall. Parchment paper is also useful, but it should be used with a wire frame. Patterned paper, including wallpapers are also useful.

Galvanised wire can be used for frames, and joins can be made with fine binding wire if they cannot be secured with solder. It is usual to attach the shade to the wire frame by silk cord or fine leather thongs. A special thonging punch can be purchased, but suitable holes can be made with a saddler's punch used with a hammer on a block of wood. Always draw lines for the thonging holes and mark off the spaces with a rule.

The pleated shade can be made with either plain or patterned paper arranged in small pleats. In measuring the material, allow 1 in. extra beyond the wire frame and double the circumference. The holes for the cords should be punched about halfway across the width of the pleat and about $\frac{3}{4}$ in. from top and bottom.

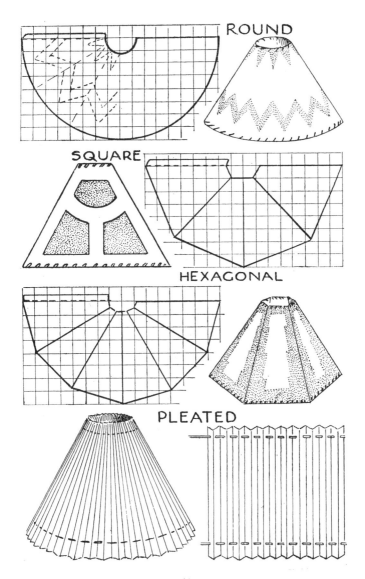

ROUND

SQUARE

HEXAGONAL

PLEATED

43

EVERLASTING FLOWER DECORATION

The bowl of flowers illustrated at the top of the next page is an example of table or window decoration made up entirely of everlasting flowers. It contains no more than four different kinds, but the great variety of colour including crimsons, yellows, pinks, purples and white with the delicate green of the stalks, give an effect of great beauty.

Not only is decoration by means of everlasting flowers an economical way of providing colourful effects, but has the advantage of being available when fresh flowers are scarce.

There is generally no difficulty in purchasing a good selection of suitable flowers from a florist, but the better plan is to grow them in the garden.

As a guide to the most suitable varieties, the following list will provide a selection suitable for all purposes. The Helichrysum: these are the large double flowers shown in the top bowl. Acrolinium provides double rose and white. Rhodanthe is a daisy like flower, the Maculata is bright rose with a white centre, the Alba variety is white, and the Manglesi is dark rose. The Xeranthemum can be grown in ordinary garden soil.

Statice, or sea lavender, is available in many beautiful pastel shades. Gypsophila is not classed as an everlasting flower, it dries well however, and is an admirable flower for use with all the flowers mentioned above.

Another most effective method of utilising everlasting flowers is to combine them with pine cones, teasle heads and sprays of honesty. An example of effective decorative treatment is shown in the lower example. In this case, the pine cones and poppy heads have been painted with a blue bronze paint and white camomile flowers after being dried were dipped in yellow and pink aniline dyes. Filling is done with statice and dried moss, also dyed in several harmonious shades.

AN EFFECTIVE ARRANGEMENT OF EVERLASTING
FLOWERS, ALL EASILY OBTAINABLE OR EASILY GROWN.

WHEN FRESH FLOWERS ARE SCARCE, USE PAINTED
PINE CONES AND POPPY HEADS WITH HONESTY AND
EVERLASTING FLOWERS AS A TABLE DECORATION.

A CLOSE WOVEN SEAT.

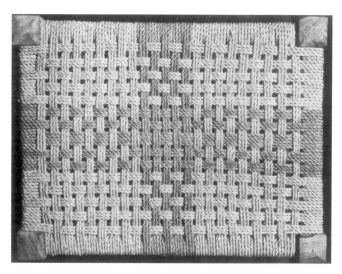

A SIMPLE METHOD OF WEAVING IN TWO COLOURS.
Photographs by Dryad Handicrafts.

46

SEATING WITH SEA-GRASS

Stool and chair seating in sea-grass is quite a simple craft. It is something that the housewife can do in spare time, but it also provides a most interesting and useful craft for either the older boys or girls.

Sea-grass is a most popular seating material, far easier than rush; it has a hard wearing surface and it is made in lengths which obviate joining. It is obtainable in a number of colours, from natural to dyed, the latter being available in orange, scarlet, indigo, dark emerald and brown. It can also be obtained in a two coloured twist in natural and orange, natural and green and brown and orange, all pleasing combinations.

Two out of a large number of different methods of weaving are shown on the previous page. For the average stool seat, from 1 lb. to $1\frac{1}{2}$ lb. is required according to the method of working. Stools can be obtained ready made in a large variety of shapes and sizes. They are made generally in birch or oak and may be finished with enamel or stained and polished without difficulty.

The methods of beginning the seating and of continuing with a pattern are shown on page 49. Before starting the actual weaving the sea-grass must be arranged in some convenient form for working. Ten yards is a convenient length and is best wound on a shuttle, which can be made quite easily from a piece of thin plywood or stout cardboard with a deep notch at each end.

The first stage consists of tying a knot close to the end of the sea-grass and tacking it on the inside of the frame as shown at the bottom of page 49. From this left-hand corner, bring the strand out under the frame, over the front rail and across the stool to the back rail. Pass it over and across the underneath of the stool to the starting point so that there is one strand on top and another underneath the frame.

Keeping the strand tight, wind the sea-grass in the same way to make a total of three strands for a simple weave, or in the case of two colours being used as shown on the next page, weave five strands. The next stage is to wrap the sea-grass once completely round the frame and then continue right across.

The second set of strands are woven across from side to side and although the method of weaving is the same, the sea-grass is carried over one set and under the next set below. It will help in this stage to thread a length of round wood as shown in the diagram just before the weaving is done. To join a new length, thread the new end through the twist of the old about 2 in. away from the end, and again 1 in. further along. Thread the old end through the twist of the new strand and the join will be secure; joins should always be on the underside of the frame. When the weaving is completed, the end is secured by tying it to one of the strands on the underside.

The pattern shown at the top of page 46 is started by a length of sea-grass to the right-hand back corner inside, carry it over on top to the back, up and round the rail close to the corner. Pass the strand across to the other side at the back, over the left rail and then up and around the back rail. The next stage is to carry it down across the open frame to the front left-hand corner over the front rail and then under and over the left rail across to the right-hand corner when it is carried over and is brought up over the front rail and carried across to the starting point.

The above method completes the first stage and the order is now followed with a second and third round and repeated until the seat is completely filled. If the seat is square, the weaving will meet in the centre as indicated, but with an oblong seat or stool, the remaining space should be filled in by working only from front to back.

Other materials for seating, such as glossy and enamelled cane can be used similarly.

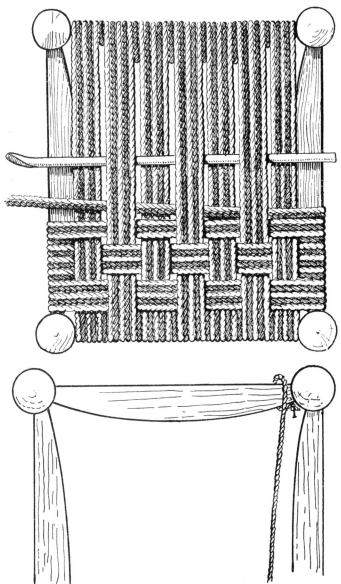

ILLUSTRATION BY DRYAD HANDICRAFTS.

RESEATING IN CANE

Six stages in recaning are shown opposite. First remove the old cane, and punch out the holes from underneath. Wash the framework with warm water and a hard brush. Begin by inserting a length of No. 2 cane in the centre hole at the back. Wedge it firmly with a peg, bring the cane to the correct hole in the front and peg it down. The cane is brought up through the next hole in front and carried to the correct hole at the back and pegged down. Continue on both sides until the whole of the seat is covered with parallel rows. With seats narrower at the back, place the cane in appropriate holes. When a join is needed bring the end up through the next hole and leave it projecting. Begin a new cane in the same way.

In stage two, the same process is followed, but the canes are across and on the top of the first lot. The third stage is a repetition of the first stage with the canes on top of the second layer. Actual weaving begins with the fourth stage, in which the cane is carried from side to side, each strand in turn being threaded over the canes of the third stage and under those of the first stage.

In the fifth stage No. 3 cane is used and it is threaded diagonally over two and under two. The sixth stage consists of diagonal threading over three and under three. Finish by driving small pegs in every alternate hole to secure the cane and prevent sagging.

To complete the caning, provide four lengths of beading cane and some fine cane for securing it in position.

Insert one end of a length of beading cane at a corner and bring it over to the next corner. Secure the length by threading the fine cane through the holes left unpegged, loop it over the beading cane and continue on all sides. Finish with a peg at the four corners to keep the beading in position.

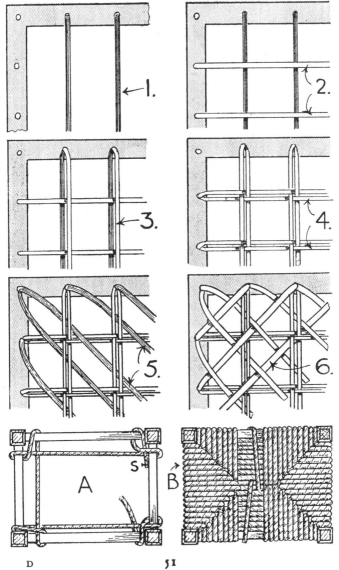

1.

2.

3.

4.

5.

6.

A

S

B

HOBBIES FOR HOUSEWIVES

Although household duties usually take up a considerable portion of the day, every housewife should endeavour to find time for practising some useful or decorative craft. Gardening is ideal for the spring and summer, but during the long winter evenings and on days when outdoor exercise is impossible, some form of light and interesting occupation will provide a pleasing contrast to the ordinary daily duties.

There are many useful little crafts eminently suitable for the housewife which do not entail much in the way of equipment or expense, quite apart from such decorative and useful work as may be carried out with the needle, knitting needles and crochet hook. It is impossible to enumerate more than a few of the most suitable of the crafts or to give detailed instructions, but as many inexpensive books are available, giving full instructions as to methods and materials, little difficulty will be found in making a beginning.

Included in the more popular of the crafts are, weaving, leatherwork, basketry, rug making, and pewter modelling. Equally suitable, are fabric printing, soft-toy making, lacquer work, gesso work, decorative dyeing, jewellery, lace making and woodcarving.

Leatherwork calls for little in the way of appliances; there is considerable choice in material and much in the way of useful work, either for household or personal use. Basketry includes the use of cane and raffia and offers scope for highly decorative as well as simple work. Pewter modelling is an inexpensive and delightful craft and with those mentioned above are opportunities for making acceptable gifts of greater value than most people can afford to buy.

Of the others mentioned, jewellery work offers opportunity for personal adornment and scope for original designs, while soft-toy making will produce articles which will be a joy to the children.

PLATE II

CURTAINS SHOULD DRAPE GRACIOUSLY AND THEIR
COLOURINGS MUST BE PERFECT.

THE CARE OF HOUSEHOLD BRUSHES

The cleaning of household brushes, including those used for the toilet, should be considered as an important household duty. Brushes, for whatever purpose they are required, should be of the best quality, cheap brushes are rarely economical, but a good quality brush, frequently washed, usually has a long life.

Brushes should be stored when not in use so that the bristles cannot be damaged, generally with the bristles uppermost. Many hair brushes are made with highly decorative backs and are intended to be placed on the dressing table with the backs uppermost. With those having fairly stiff fibres it does not matter if the fibres are downwards, but with soft brushes, it is advisable to keep them in a drawer, protected from dust.

The household sweeping brushes should be suspended on pegs in a special brush cupboard if possible; if inconvenient to stand them upright or have the bristles on top, they should be suspended bristles downwards, but not allowed to touch the floor.

Hair brushes and others used for the toilet should be washed from time to time in warm water with soap flakes and a little ammonia. First remove hair and fluff with a comb and wash them in a lather. Rinse thoroughly in warm water, shake to remove surplus moisture and place in a draughty position to dry.

Household brushes should also be washed in warm water and soap flakes. Soda or strong soaps should not be used. The lather should be rubbed thoroughly into the bristles and when clean the brush should be rinsed in warm water.

Brushes used for painting or varnishing should be cleaned with turpentine. Those used for cellulose paint must be cleaned in the solvent advised or with amyl acetate. After cleaning with turps., etc., the brush should be washed with soap and water, rinsed and then dried. When dry, paint brushes should be wrapped in paper.

MINIATURE TABLE GARDENS

Two typical Japanese gardens are illustrated on the next page. They are obtainable in various sizes and are furnished with dwarfed trees, pagodas and other quaint buildings, bridges, lakes, birds, animals and figures, at a reasonable figure, and with care will last for years. When purchasing ready-made Japanese gardens, go to a reputable firm.

Miniature gardens can be made quite easily and inexpensively with materials to be found in the countryside or purchased at the florists and oriental stores. They should be built in an earthenware baking dish to any convenient size, one measuring 12 in. by 7 in. is suitable for a start.

Collect the materials first—sandstone and granite chips will provide rock material, the shell gravel used for bird cages will do for paths. Suitable foliage can be supplied from mosses, tufts of grass, cactus of various kinds, seedling oaks and beeches from the woods or hillside, sprigs of heather and tiny ferns.

Pagodas, bridges and small buildings are easily made, but these can be purchased from the stores as well as suitable birds and figures. Lakes can be formed by saucers or glass dishes : much ingenuity can be expended in making up a garden, and it is fascinating work.

Growing plants should be gathered with the original soil covering the roots and planted in well sifted soil, which should more or less fill the dish. Press the soil firmly, arrange the buildings, etc., and then finish with moss where desired. Genuine stunted trees are expensive, due to the care required in their cultivation.

As the dish used for the garden will not allow of drainage, it is a good plan to line the bottom with sharp gravel or stone chips before filling with soil. The latter should be kept moist but not really wet, and from time to time all the growing foliage should be sprayed, preferably with rain water.

GARDENS IN MINIATURE.

Photographs by Liberty & Co., Ltd.

BULBS GROWN IN POTS FILLED WITH PREPARED FIBRE.

GRASS SEED SOWN IN THE FIBRE MAKES AN EFFECTIVE
CARPET FOR THE BULBS.

BULBS IN BOWLS

The cultivation of bulbs provides for flowers at a time when cut flowers are difficult to obtain. The hyacinth with its variety in colouring is always popular; daffodils, narcissus and tulips are quite as easily grown, and the begonia, with its brilliant colouring, should not be overlooked.

For indoor cultivation it is advisable to purchase bulbs of first quality and to use prepared fibre for use in the bowls. Suitable bowls are inexpensive and are available in a number of shapes and sizes. Generally, in a bowl measuring about 7 in. in diameter and 3 in. deep, it is possible to grow three hyacinths or four or five daffodils or tulips.

The prepared fibre, which should contain a small amount of charcoal, should be carefully powdered and placed in a large bowl or clean pail. Add water, preferably rain water, to make the fibre thoroughly wet and then line each bowl about halfway up. Select the bulbs carefully and place in position, not too near the edge of the bowl and well separated. Fill up the bowl with the wet fibre but do not quite cover the tops of the bulbs.

The bowls are now placed in a cool airy place; there is no need to keep them entirely in the dark, but they should be left alone until the growth begins, when they can be brought gradually in the full light and by degrees into more warmth.

The appearance of the bowls can be enhanced by sowing fine grass around the bulbs. As soon as the growth is a few inches high, sprinkle some fine grass seed on the fibre and press it lightly; in a short time the grass will sprout and by the time the bulbs are in flower the grass will be 2 in. or 3 in. high and will hide the bulb entirely. Bulbs require little moisture until they are well grown, and then should be watered regularly.

As soon as the bulbs have flowered, they should be taken out and either planted in the garden or stored.

A BULB BASKET

The usual method of growing bulbs is to use an earthenware bowl, but bulbs can be grown in almost any kind of utensil. Old coal scuttles, pans of all kinds, basins or vegetable dishes, in fact, anything large enough to hold the necessary fibre in which the bulb should be embedded. The children should be encouraged to grow bulbs for their own rooms, and, if suitable bowls are not available, baskets can be made from waste materials, or old baskets can be put into a passable state of repair and when suitably lined will grow bulbs admirably. The bulb basket shown on the next page is one of many useful jobs for the boy or girl who likes using a saw, hammer and nails. It is a page from "101 Things for Little Folks to Do."

Begin with a piece of wood $\frac{1}{4}$ in. thick and about $3\frac{1}{2}$ in. square, and cut off the corners so that they are all equal. Now get some lengths of round wood and saw them to a length of 3 in. Split the lengths down the centre and nail them on the sides of the wood, leaving $\frac{1}{2}$ in. projecting from the bottom.

The next thing is to find a pliable twig to bend into a ring so that it can be nailed to the top of the uprights as shown in the middle drawing. Be very careful to avoid splitting the upright pieces when nailing. Use fine nails and leave them projecting a little way as shown.

The outside has to be closely wrapped in some sort of fibre, rush for example. If Michaelmas daisies are in the garden, or easily procured, use the stalks after soaking them. Last of all, wrap some fine wire round the nails and behind the feet as shown in the bottom diagram, and then hammer the top nails down close to the band. The fibres and wood can be coated with varnish if it is handy.

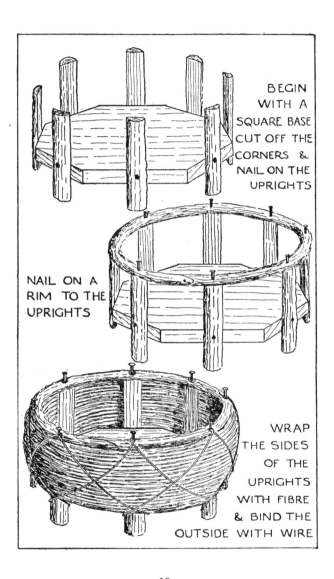

BEGIN
WITH A
SQUARE BASE
CUT OFF THE
CORNERS &
NAIL ON THE
UPRIGHTS

NAIL ON A
RIM TO THE
UPRIGHTS

WRAP
THE SIDES
OF THE
UPRIGHTS
WITH FIBRE
& BIND THE
OUTSIDE WITH WIRE

WINDOW GARDENING

Dwellers in flats and apartments are often denied the pleasures of cultivating flowers in the open ground, and are compelled to rely on the small spaces provided by the window sill. With care and attention, window boxes can be used to provide flowers from seed and also to hold flowers in pots.

The ideal window box is one specially made from wood about 1 in. thick, to fit the exact space available, but it is quite possible to join a number of small boxes together and make a satisfactory garden. Usually the space available does not exceed 9 in. and in this case only comparatively narrow boxes are suitable; they should be as deep as possible, not less than 5 in.

It is impossible to give more than a rough guide to the arrangement of the boxes. First the slope of the sill must be considered; this can be overcome by nailing the boxes to a stout board to rest on the front of the sill. If the latter should be narrow, the boxes should be supported underneath with a suitable strip of wood.

One of the essentials in the construction of a window box is to provide for drainage. In some cases it may be necessary to prevent water draining from the box from running down the wall; in this case it will be necessary to fit a zinc tray on the sill, but in every box holes should be bored in the bottom. For holding flower-pots only, the bottom of the boxes should be covered with a layer of ashes; in boxes to be filled with soil, the bottom layer should be composed of broken pieces of old flower pots.

If the separate boxes are held together in front with a board, the latter may be relieved by small pieces of wood nailed on to give a panelled effect. Before being used, all the wood should be given at least two coats of paint. A simple method of attaching the window box is to use angle brackets; these are easily screwed to the top of each end box and to the window frame.

WINDOW GARDENING.

BORE HOLES
FOR DRAINAGE
COVER WITH
BROKEN CROCKS

PLAIN BOXES WILL DO

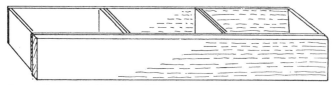

BOXES NAILED TO A FRONT BOARD

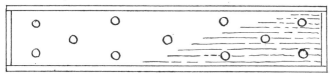

DRAINAGE HOLES IN WINDOW BOX

FRONT OF BOARD PANELLED

ANGLE BRACKET
ATTACHMENT

EXTRA SHELVES IN THE PANTRY

Usually there are not enough shelves in the pantry to store all the various bottles, jars, tins, etc., in such a position that they can be seen at a glance. As a rule it is unnecessary to have more than one deep shelf, but it is convenient to have a number of narrow shelves on which single rows of articles may be arranged.

The illustration on the next page shows a typical cupboard or pantry fitted with a number of extra shelves easily made from boxes and plywood strips. In addition, suggestions are given for the provision of hooks on the inside of the door as well as a wire letter cage for use in storing vegetables, etc.

The plywood strips on the top shelf need not be more than 3 in. or 4 in. wide ; they are supported on uprights cut from the same material as the shelves to which they are nailed. Unless heavy articles are placed on the top of these shelves, there is no need to nail on a back piece, but if necessary a strip of the same material nailed to the back will make the shelves perfectly rigid.

Narrow shelves, made of 3 in. by $\frac{1}{2}$ in. wood, can be attached to the wall in any required position by means of brass mirror or glass plates ; the latter are screwed to the back of the shelves and attached to the wall with fairly stout wire nails. These shelves should be used only for light articles.

Light packing cases or similar boxes can be arranged at the back of the deep shelf. A simple method is to place the boxes at the back and sides of the slab.

Extra shelves underneath the deep shelf or slab should be made from boards about $\frac{3}{4}$ in. thick, and rested on supports of 2 in. by 1 in. wood attached to the wall with stout cut nails. The arrangement of hooks on the inside of the door should be made to suit individual requirements. As a rule it will be necessary to fit strips between the door stiles to prevent the screws being driven through the panel.

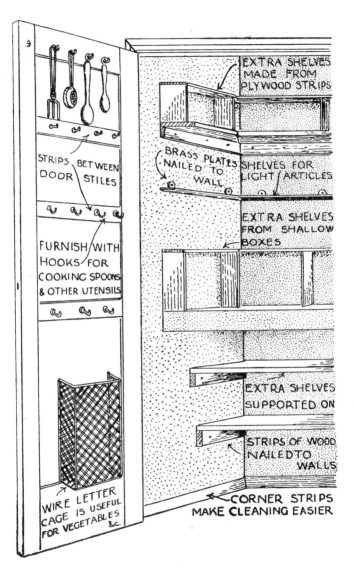

STRIPS BETWEEN DOOR STILES

FURNISH WITH HOOKS FOR COOKING SPOONS & OTHER UTENSILS

WIRE LETTER CAGE IS USEFUL FOR VEGETABLES &c.

EXTRA SHELVES MADE FROM PLYWOOD STRIPS

BRASS PLATES NAILED TO WALL

SHELVES FOR LIGHT ARTICLES

EXTRA SHELVES FROM SHALLOW BOXES

EXTRA SHELVES SUPPORTED ON

STRIPS OF WOOD NAILED TO WALLS

CORNER STRIPS MAKE CLEANING EASIER

CARE OF REFRIGERATORS

There are two main types of mechanical refrigerator: one is actuated by gas and the other by an electric motor.

The refrigerator forms the ideal larder, it is dust-proof, fly-proof, heat-proof and damp-proof. It keeps perishable food fresh and wholesome, milk and cream always fresh and it prevents household waste.

The remarkable growth in the number of electrically-driven and gas refrigerators during recent years has proved their value as a necessary article of household equipment. Although the initial cost of a refrigerator is somewhat high, special terms of purchase are available. The refrigerator should be considered as a means towards obtaining wholesome and uncontaminated food.

The gas refrigerator illustrated on the next page is most economical to run, it requires just a tiny gas flame, there are no moving parts and, therefore, permanent silence and no radio interference.

To obtain the best results from a mechanical refrigerator, the shelves and the interior should be kept perfectly clean. The contents should be checked daily and spills wiped up. Once a week the interior should be wiped clean, especially the shelves. The ice trays should be emptied and refilled regularly.

The vegetable and salad container should be attended to frequently to prevent excessive moisture and the maker's instructions regarding de-frosting should not be neglected. This should be done about every fortnight; if left too long without de-frosting, the cooling unit becomes so heavily coated with ice that its efficiency is greatly reduced.

With electrically run refrigerators, it is necessary to oil the bearings of the motor periodically; instructions are provided by the makers and should be carefully noted. Actually, there is no difference between the two types so far as interior cleaning is concerned, they are both effective in use.

AN ELECTROLUX GAS REFRIGERATOR.

EASILY MADE SHELVES FOR THE KITCHEN.

66

FITTING KITCHEN SHELVES

With the possibilities that exist for obtaining ready planed wood to almost any width and thickness, the housewife who can use a saw, a hammer and screwdriver should have little difficulty in making shelves.

A suggestion is given on the previous page for an easily made set of shelves to carry plates, dishes, cups and saucers, and jugs. The example shown was made to fit in a narrow space between two doors in a small kitchen so that the small dresser could be used for the storage of other articles of daily use.

In the example given, the wood used was finished to 4 in. wide and $\frac{3}{8}$ in. thick, the two upright sides are 3 ft. 6 in. long. The three shelves made up the width to fit the available space of 2 ft. 10 in. The front lower corners of the upright pieces were rounded by sawing off the corner and then the wood was smoothed on the sawn edges with a file. The position of the shelves should be marked off on both of the uprights placed edge to edge, careful measurements being made on both outside edges. The lowest shelf is 4 in. up, a line above at a distance of $\frac{3}{8}$ in. gives the position of the top of the shelf. The next two are 11 in. above the top of the shelf immediately below.

For nailing, draw a line to indicate the centre of the shelf thickness and then drive four 2 in. wire nails through both upright sides into each shelf. Keep the nails quite upright and if the tool is available, use a punch so that the head of each nail can be driven just below the surface. The nail holes can be filled in with plastic wood before the shelf is painted. The shelves should be finished with two coats of white paint or enamel.

In the example, the shelf was nailed to the architraves of the doors, but if this is not possible, two brass mirror or glass plates, can be screwed to the back of the top and bottom shelves so that nails can be driven through into the wall; use Rawlplugs in a soft wall.

EASILY MADE WINDOW SEAT

The attractive window seat shown on the next page can be made by the housewife with two or three suitable boxes, some strips of wood and some plywood. The hangings and the cushions are simple. Although the illustrations show a method of dealing with a square cornered recess, it is a simple matter to fill in a recess having a considerably wider angle.

It will be seen in the lower diagram that suitable boxes must be provided; a height from 12 in. to 15 in. will do, the boxes therefore should be the required width or height. The number of boxes will depend on the length of the recess. The top, made of plywood, should be measured off and either one or two lengths provided; these can be obtained cut ready to size. A few nails driven through the plywood into the upright portions of the boxes, as indicated by the arrow heads, will keep the seat together.

If the plywood top should project beyond the ends of the boxes owing to the outward splay of the walls of the recess, it will be necessary to provide a support; either an extra box should be taken apart and the ends fitted against the wall, or a suitable strip, say about 2 in. by 1 in., nailed to the wall on each side.

The curtains and pelmet, if required, can be suspended from a length of brass or iron rod resting on the picture rail as shown, or secured to the wall with screw eyes. The drapery at the back of the seat can be cut to the required depth, sewn to Rufflette tape, and either tacked at intervals to a strip of wood nailed to the wall under the shelf or window frame, or it can be threaded on a length of brass or iron rod, the latter being held in position with screw eyes. The same method can be applied to the drapery in front of the boxes. The cushions can be made from spring units and provided with suitable covers to a thickness of from 3 in. to 4 in. Suggestions for making cushions are given on page 94.

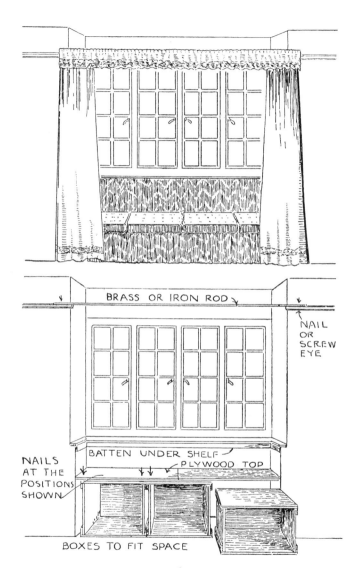

BRASS OR IRON ROD

NAIL
OR
SCREW
EYE

NAILS
AT THE
POSITIONS
SHOWN

BATTEN UNDER SHELF

PLYWOOD TOP

BOXES TO FIT SPACE

69

MAKING A MODERN DIVAN BED

During recent years the divan bed has become popular ; the wooden and the brass bedstead with its high framework does not lend itself to modern ideas. Although the adaption of the metal framed bedstead is more difficult, the work of transforming a wooden bedstead to conform with modern conditions is simple.

A suggestion is given on the next page for modernising the ordinary wooden bedstead by cutting down the tall head to replace the usually lower foot, the latter being instead used as the head. First dismantle the bedstead and remove the side bed irons, and take off the brackets from the head piece. Next saw down the lower portion of the wooden frame to a convenient height, from 2 ft. to 2 ft. 6 in. Remove the castors and replace, measure the correct height for the brackets, screw them on in their new position and then fit the side irons.

Bedsteads with solid ends or with curved tops are not quite so easy to alter, but usually there is some portion of the framework at which the sawing can be done. Care must be taken that shortening does not weaken the construction.

As a rule it is advisable to leave the brass bedstead alone, but the plain iron bedstead as indicated at the bottom of the next page can be modernised by covering the head and foot with a casing of wood. No constructional alterations are needed in regard to the iron framework, the latter being first covered on the outside with lengths of $1\frac{1}{2}$ in. by $\frac{3}{4}$ in. wood fitted closely to sides and top. The upright lengths should be about 1 in. from the floor to allow for the castors. Cover the outside of the wooden frame with plywood at both ends. The inside, head and foot, should be covered as far as the side irons top and bottom. The plywood should be fixed with screws, either flush with the frame or allowed to project sufficiently to allow for strips of plywood to cover the frame.

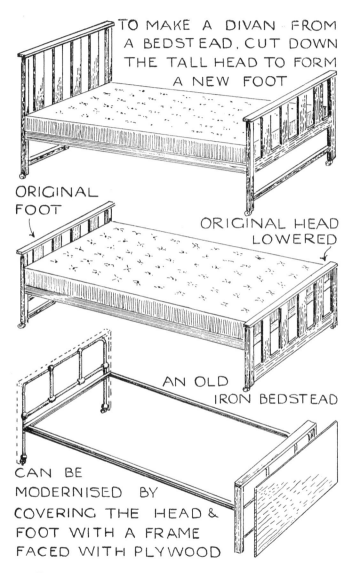

TO MAKE A DIVAN FROM
A BEDSTEAD, CUT DOWN
THE TALL HEAD TO FORM
A NEW FOOT

ORIGINAL
FOOT

ORIGINAL HEAD
LOWERED

AN OLD
IRON BEDSTEAD

CAN BE
MODERNISED BY
COVERING THE HEAD &
FOOT WITH A FRAME
FACED WITH PLYWOOD

FITTING A NEW WASHER

A dripping tap or faucet is not only annoying but it is wasteful; the cure is easily effected by fitting a new washer. All ordinary taps are made in three parts comprising the supply pipe, otherwise the spout, the stem and nut combined, and the washer which is attached to a plug or jumper.

First of all, the position of the main stop-cock should be discovered, and the main water supply must be shut off. In modern plumbing, it is usual to fit a stop-cock inside the house at some convenient place, otherwise it will be necessary to shut off the supply at the point outside the house where it is attached to the inside main supply. Now turn on the tap and drain off the water; this is also necessary to make sure that the supply is disconnected.

The next job is to loosen the big nut around the stem: this must be done with a spanner or monkey-wrench. Take out the stem and remove the plug or jumper. The washer, which may be rubber, leather or composition, is usually attached to the plug with a small nut; remove this and fit on a new washer. Before replacing the washer, examine the inside of the tap to see that none of the old washer remains, then fit in the plug, replace the stem and tighten up the big nut, using the monkey-wrench to turn it, and making it as tight as possible. Finally turn on the main supply and turn off the tap.

Some modern taps, as shown in the diagram, have a metal casing over the large nut attached to the stem. So that sufficient room can be provided for the wrench, it will be necessary to undo the stem and open the tap fully, the shield or cover is now unscrewed and lifted up the stem. When dealing with a tap attached to the hot-water system, unless a special stop-cock has been provided, it will be necessary to empty the hot-water tank before a new washer can be fitted.

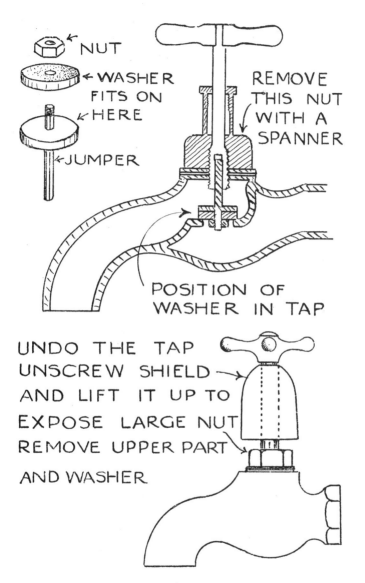

NUT

WASHER
FITS ON
HERE

JUMPER

REMOVE
THIS NUT
WITH A
SPANNER

POSITION OF
WASHER IN TAP

UNDO THE TAP
UNSCREW SHIELD
AND LIFT IT UP TO
EXPOSE LARGE NUT
REMOVE UPPER PART
AND WASHER

MENDING ELECTRIC CORDS OR FLEX

Electric cords and flex are used to connect the electric iron, the bowl, the heater and other appliances to the power plug. They should in all cases be kept dry and in good condition, and they must be unbroken. With continual use, it often happens that one or more of the connections may break off and the flow of current will cease. In most cases, a sudden breakage will cause a fuse to blow out.

First of all disconnect the cord from the supply, not by pulling the cord, but by gripping the plug firmly and withdrawing the pins from the power point. It should be noted that carelessness in disconnecting the supply by pulling the cord instead of the plug is a frequent cause of damage.

There are a number of devices which act as plugs, but in the main it will be found that the two wires from the cord are attached to the plug by small screws. Examine the plug carefully and then undo the screw or screws which keep the cover or cap in position. Give the screws inside a turn or two to release any attached wire and then turn the screws back far enough to free the small holes entirely.

Examine the end of the cord and cut away sufficient of the outside insulating covering to expose enough of the twin wires to fit inside the plug. Note that the twin wires are also covered with insulating rubber; enough of the covering should be removed to leave at least $\frac{1}{2}$ in. of bare wire. Now twist the fine strands of wire together and fold over as shown, twist up tightly, insert in the holes provided and then screw up, leaving no stray portions of wire exposed. Finally screw on the cap and the plug is ready to insert into the point.

In the course of time, electric cords are liable to deterioration caused by the hardening of the insulation. It is essential that all such means of supply should be examined periodically and if necessary renewed.

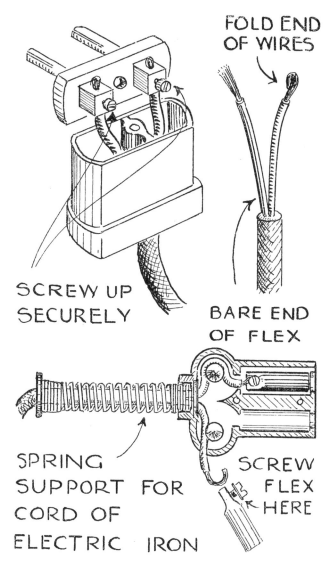

FOLD END
OF WIRES

SCREW UP
SECURELY

BARE END
OF FLEX

SPRING
SUPPORT FOR
CORD OF
ELECTRIC IRON

SCREW
FLEX
HERE

RENEWING A BURNT-OUT FUSE

The fuse is a safety device which " blows out " when the current is overloaded. Sometimes the addition of a toaster or an electric iron to an already overworked circuit will blow out a fuse and often a similar appliance or a bowl fire attached to an already overloaded lighting circuit will be sufficient to overload it. A defective plug or a damaged flex or cord will cause a short circuit resulting in an abnormally large flow of current which will also melt the fuse.

Actually, the fuse is a fine wire attached to two contact plates which fit in a specially designed appliance known as the fuse box. Usually the fuse box is situated close to the main supply meter, and it contains a number of removable sockets each connected with a separate circuit. It is usual to have separate fuse boxes for the lighting and the heating circuits. The circuit is the wiring to and from the main supply to which are attached the lamp sockets for lighting, or in the case of heating or power, the fires or other appliances using a high consumption of current.

The first thing to do when the fuse blows is to turn off the main switch, so that all current is cut off; this is most important and should on no account be neglected. Next open the box and withdraw the sockets one by one until the one containing the burnt out wire is discovered. The operation of renewing the wire is a simple job, and consists of undoing the connecting screws, removing the burnt ends of the old wire and wiping the porcelain quite clean. Cut off a suitable length and, if necessary, straighten it out.

The correct fuse wire to use depends on the voltage of the main supply and on the particular circuit. The size of the wire is reckoned in amps and the correct gauge should be ascertained from the source of the supply. Having procured the wire, attach it to the screws as indicated, replace the socket and finally turn on the current.

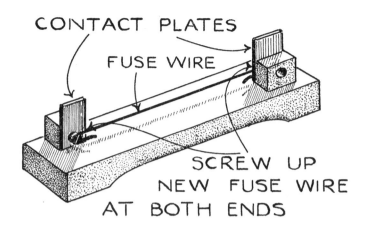

CONTACT PLATES

FUSE WIRE

SCREW UP
NEW FUSE WIRE
AT BOTH ENDS

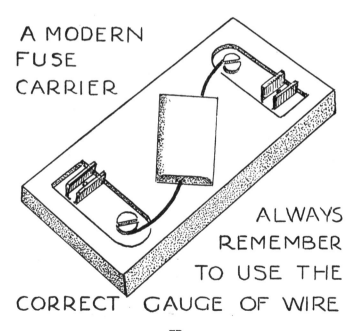

A MODERN
FUSE
CARRIER

ALWAYS
REMEMBER
TO USE THE
CORRECT GAUGE OF WIRE

READING THE METERS

The economical housewife should keep a careful check on the consumption of electricity and gas, and this can be done by reading the dials of the meters. Within the capacity of the circuit, it does not matter how many of the lights are burning at one time, but if extra lights or small appliances such as an electric iron, a toaster or even a small bowl fire should be at any time added to the circuit, it is probable that the circuit would become overloaded and the fuse would blow out. This point should be watched carefully, and as a rule, no more than the usual load should be allowed.

Electricity is measured by a meter which indicates the number of watts used. The watt is a small unit and the distributing unit is the kilowatt, or 1,000 watts. The dials on the front of the meter register 10 ; 100 ; 1,000 and 10,000. In the example shown on the next page, the right-hand dial reads 80, the next 300, which plus the 80 shows 380. The third indicates 5,000, giving 5,380, and the last one, having just passed the index 1, shows a total consumption of 15,380. The charge for each distributing unit varies with the supply, but knowing the charge per unit, the cost can be estimated

Gas, although not greatly used for lighting, is still in everyday use for cooking and heating. It is distributed through pipes and although not subject to troubles connected with overloading and blown fuses, it is necessary to prevent leakage which, if not remedied, may lead to serious explosions. The meter to register the consumption of gas indicates cubic feet ; there are generally three dials, the dial on the right measures 100 feet, the next one indicates 1,000's and the third 10,000 feet. The meter reading as shown on the next page, reads 400, 9,000 and 70,000, altogether 79,400. When the indicator is between numbers, the lesser number is taken. The charges are by feet or a number of feet, indicated by a therm.

METER DIALS

ELECTRIC METER READING 1538 Kw

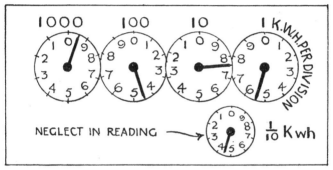

1000   100   10   1 K.W.H. PER DIVISION

NEGLECT IN READING →   1/10 Kwh

ELECTRIC METER READING
          9475 KILOWATTS

100 THOUSAND   10 THOUSAND   1 THOUSAND

GAS METER READING
    61400 CUBIC FEET

USING THERMOMETERS

There are two kinds of thermometers which should be in every household, one to measure the heat of the atmosphere, or of water and other liquids, and is mounted usually on a wood or metal support, the other is used to measure the heat of the body and is known as a clinical thermometer. This is a plain glass tube and is kept in a metal case when not in use.

Heat on a thermometer is measured by degrees and there are two scales in ordinary use ; Fahrenheit gives the freezing point at 32° and boiling point at 220°. The Centigrade scale has the freezing point at o, with the boiling point at 100°. The former is in use generally.

A bath thermometer, usually enclosed in a wooden case, as shown on the next page, should be part of a normal bathroom equipment, and is specially useful in obtaining a suitable temperature for children's baths. Metal cased thermometers are also useful for gauging the heat of an oven when cooking.

Some thermometers are arranged to show the maximum and the minimum temperatures and require adjustment from time to time. The most useful form for the household has either a mercury or alcohol filled tube ; the scale indications show freezing point at 32°, temperate heat at 60°, and summer heat at 76°.

A suitable indoor temperature is 65°, and as far as possible the temperature inside the house should not greatly exceed this reading. Although many people are accustomed to keep rooms at a higher temperature, it is far healthier to avoid overheated rooms.

The clinical thermometer is used in illness ; the scale usually runs from about 95° to 110°, with an arrow mark to indicate normal blood heat which is just above 98°. The degrees are divided into five parts and the temperature is read by degrees and points. After use clinical thermometers should be dipped in an antiseptic solution, dried and the mercury shaken down.

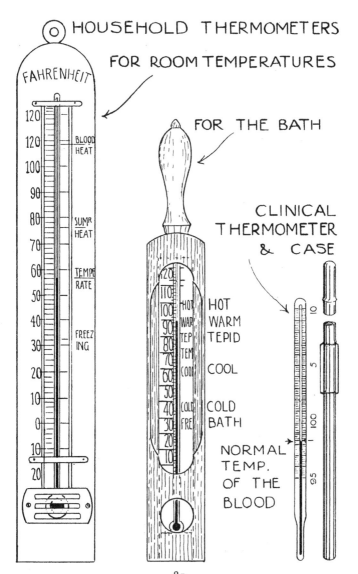

HOUSEHOLD THERMOMETERS
FOR ROOM TEMPERATURES

FAHRENHEIT

120
120   BLOOD HEAT
100
90
80   SUMR HEAT
70
60   TEMPE RATE
50
40
30   FREEZ ING
20
10
0
10
20

FOR THE BATH

CLINICAL THERMOMETER & CASE

120 F
110
100   HOT   HOT
90   WAR   WARM
  TEP   TEPID
80   TEM
70
60   COO   COOL
50
40   COLD   COLD
30   FRE   BATH
20
10

NORMAL TEMP. OF THE BLOOD

10
5
100
95

WEIGHTS AND MEASURES

Household scales are an important part of the kitchen equipment. The ordinary old-fashioned balance with its range of weights is not so convenient as the lever spring balance with a large dial. Apart from the compactness of the latter appliance, the adjusting screw will allow of bowls and plates with their contents to be weighed instead of placing everything on the pan. The receptacle can be weighed first or its weight allowed for by means of the adjusting screw.

There are many equivalents to weights and measures, especially the latter; a knowledge of them will save time in the kitchen. For example, 3 teaspoonfuls make one tablespoonful, 16 tablespoonfuls make one cup. The contents of a cup measure 8 fluid ounces, 2 cups make a pint and 2 pints make a quart; or 4 gills make a pint, and 2 pints make a quart. In any case these measurements are only approximate, but answer for plain cooking. In order to obtain uniformity in measurement, it is advisable to keep a special spoon and cup and in using them, level off or fill to the brim.

The weights of various materials differ considerably. For example, 2 cups of granulated sugar weigh approximately 1 lb., while a similar quantity of flour weighs about $\frac{1}{2}$ lb. A level tablespoonful of liquid weighs about $\frac{1}{2}$ oz., the same weight in sugar and butter can be gauged by the same measure.

Metric measurements are often quoted and a list of equivalents will be found useful. The centimetre is just under one-third of an inch, a metre is just over 1 yard. A litre measures a little less than a quart and a metric gram is a trifle less than a third of an ounce. All these measurements are approximate only.

Measures of length should, as a rule, be made with a tape measure or a yard stick. A square yard measures 3 ft. each way, and contains 9 sq. ft., and each square foot contains 144 square inches.

HOUSEHOLD
SCALES

SPRING
BALANCE

THE WEIGHTS
CANNOT BE
MISLAID

SPRING
BALANCE
FOR PARCELS

QUART
& PINT MILK BOTTLES

PINT
MEASURE

$\frac{1}{2}$ PINT
CUP

HAT WARDROBE

The hat wardrobe illustrated on the next page is easily made and provides a useful fitment; it can be suspended from a convenient hook or placed on the floor in a corner of the room. It is made from discs of cardboard or plywood supported by lengths of prepared dowelling.

Provide four 36 in. long dowels about $\frac{3}{8}$ in. diameter and four circular pieces of stout cardboard, millboard, or thin plywood cut to a diameter of approximately 12 in. Divide the outside of the circles into four equal parts and then nail the top and bottom pieces to the lengths of dowel. If possible the top and bottom pieces should be plywood, with cardboard inner discs.

Divide the height into three equal parts, bind some wire from side to side, cut out slots in the circumference of the discs and fit them inside the uprights. Bind some fairly stout wire about 1 in. below and above the top and bottom pieces respectively to provide means for attaching the fabric cover. The opening should be a section between two uprights and the material fastened to small rings which can be threaded on the wires.

SHOE TIDY

The illustration at the bottom of the next page shows an easily made shoe tidy intended for attaching to the lower position of the bedroom door. The material used can be of any suitable fabric such as cretonne and the back piece should be made to the full width of the door and about 12 in. deep. On all sides provide a hem to take suitable length of $\frac{3}{8}$ in. or $\frac{1}{2}$ in. diameter dowels which should meet at the corners.

The width of the pockets should be at least 6 in., but the actual size depends on the width of the door and it may be possible to arrange for more than four pockets.

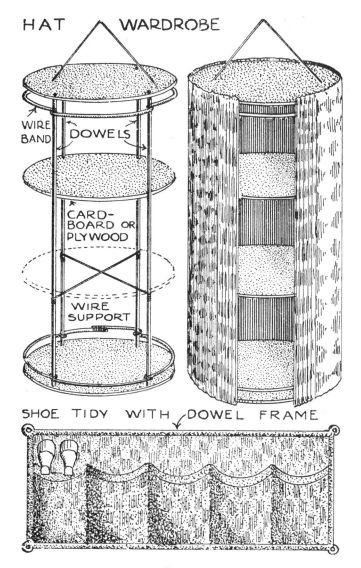

HAT WARDROBE

WIRE BAND

DOWELS

CARD-BOARD OR PLYWOOD

WIRE SUPPORT

SHOE TIDY WITH DOWEL FRAME

MAKING WASTEPAPER BASKETS

Although the term basket is usually applied to receptacles made of osier and cane, it can be used generally to describe any form of container for waste paper. It is convenient to provide a place for depositing waste paper and odds and ends in every room. Several suggestions for simple boxes are shown.

Empty biscuit boxes suitably painted and decorated make excellent receptacles. The paper covering should be stripped off and the surfaces, both inside and out, thoroughly washed. For painting use an enamel or a cellulose paint, but apply a preliminary coat of ordinary paint as an undercoat which should be rubbed down smooth with pumice powder or glasspaper when quite dry. Decoration can be stencilled.

Wood boxes can be made from suitable pieces of plywood which can be nailed with panel pins or glued and nailed to a triangular fillet of wood at each corner. The plywood can be painted or stained with an oil varnish stain to match the furniture in the room. Another form of basket can be made from lengths of dowelling. These are obtained in a number of thicknesses : one about $\frac{1}{2}$ in. diameter is convenient. The dowels should be cut to a length of 12 in. or so, holes are bored with a gimlet about 1 in. or so from the ends and then the lengths are threaded on lengths of wire with suitable wooden beads in between. The dowels and the beads can be enamelled before threading. The bottom can be made from a tin lid, plywood or millboard. The inside should be lined with cretonne or other material.

Cardboard is also suitable. Panels should be cut to size and may be covered entirely with paper or fabric. Ordinary flour paste is a convenient adhesive. In the shape shown at the bottom of the page, the six panels are separately covered, holes punched on the sides to allow for lacing with cord as indicated.

FOR THE WASTE PAPER.

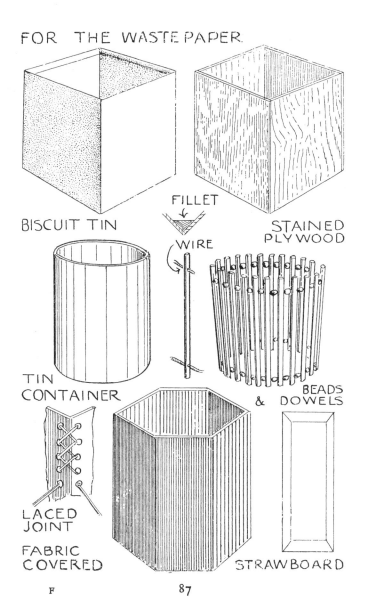

BISCUIT TIN

FILLET

WIRE

STAINED
PLYWOOD

TIN
CONTAINER

BEADS
& DOWELS

LACED
JOINT

FABRIC
COVERED

STRAWBOARD

UPHOLSTERED BOXES

The upholstered box shown on the next page is quite easily made, and besides forming a small footstool or pouffe, can be used as a receptacle for needlework or slippers. The material used for covering the box can be similar to that used for loose covers, and provides a useful means of utilising odd pieces.

An ordinary small packing case of a suitable size makes an excellent box for the purpose. It will be necessary to provide a top which can be hinged to one side of the case. A piece of plywood at least $\frac{1}{2}$ in. thick should be used. In addition the ends of the case, if of the particular kind shown, should be filled in with wood or any suitable packing. The hinges can be screwed as shown on the outside edge of the lid and the case.

The top can be padded with curled hair ; an excellent material is that known as hairlok, it is a mixture of hair and rubber, forming a springy pad. There are many suitable forms of filling, but for lasting wear, hair is best. The filling should be distributed evenly on the surface to a thickness of about 2 in. and covered with hessian or canvas tacked down on all edges.

There are several ways of attaching the fabric to the sides of the case : in the illustration on the next page, the material is folded over top and bottom. It should be carried completely round the case and secured on all edges. Fabric covered studs can be used, but the material can be tacked on with gimp pins.

If the extra work and material is not an objection, it is worth while covering the sides and the padded top with upholsterer's wadding. At least one layer should be used under the covering material. It will be found a convenience to fix some kind of castor on the bottom of the box. Wheel castors can be used, but a good quality ball castor will be found more satisfactory. They are easily attached with screws. The finished box can be lined with paper or glazed cloth pasted on.

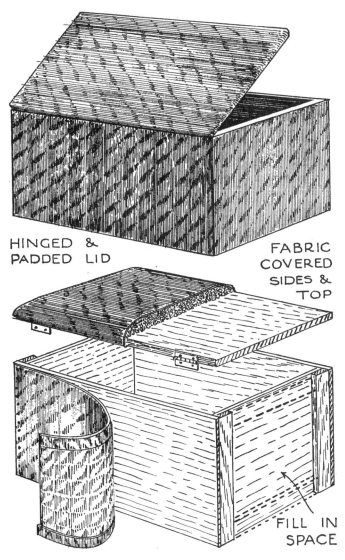

HINGED &
PADDED LID

FABRIC
COVERED
SIDES &
TOP

FILL IN
SPACE

89

CARE OF THE SEWING MACHINE

In order to obtain the best results from the use of a sewing machine, it must, like all pieces of machinery, be kept in good condition. Oiling should be done periodically, and when not in use the machine should be covered and protected from dust. When it is in use a certain amount of dust will work its way into the bearings, and from time to time all accessible parts should be wiped clean with an oily rag.

Manufacturers of sewing machines usually provide a handbook giving full instructions as to oiling and cleaning and supply a special oil or recommend a suitable brand. The special oil known as " Three-in-One " is ideal for machines, as it prevents rust as well as lubricates. On no account should thick lubricating oil be used.

If a machine has been neglected or has not been in use for a long time, it is possible that the oil in some of the working parts has become oxidised and hardened. The remedy is to brush all the parts, both inside and out, with paraffin, wipe clean and then apply new oil. It is an advantage to remove the needle and run the machine for some time to allow the oil to work into the bearings.

A good sewing machine rarely gives trouble and when troubles do occur, they can be traced to faults in adjustment. Attention should be paid to correct tension, to winding bobbins correctly, to use of good cotton or silk, and to see that the needle is suitable for the material and a correct one for the particular make of machine.

For occasional use the hand machine will be found to give every satisfaction, but greater ease in working can be obtained with a treadle machine, examples of both machines are shown on the next page. A modern improvement which removes most of the laborious work in machining is embodied in the treadle machine illustrated : it consists of a small electric motor drive together with an electric light which illuminates the needle. This attachment is equally suitable for the hand machine.

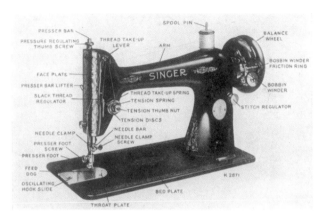

THE MAIN PARTS OF A SEWING MACHINE.

Photographs of Singer Sewing Machines.

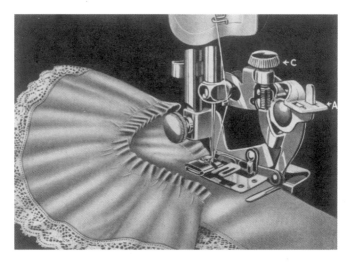

THE RUFFLER ATTACHMENT IN USE.

PHOTOGRAPHS OF THE RUFFLER ATTACHMENT
SUPPLIED FOR USE WITH A SINGER SEWING
MACHINE.

92

USING SEWING MACHINE ATTACHMENTS

Bindings of various materials can be applied with the Binder attachment. This attachment folds and guides the binding, and by a simple adjustment the stitching can be regulated to come close to the edge of the binding. Binding suitably applied, forms a trimming for washable dresses, children's clothes, underwear and articles for home decoration.

The *Foot Hemmer* and the adjustable hemmer may be used for a variety of purposes. Hemming of all widths is easily done and hemming and the sewing of a lace edge can be carried out in one operation. This is one of the most useful of the available attachments.

Another useful attachment is the *Tucker*. Tucks may be made in any width, from a fine pin tuck to one inch wide ; they form a natural trimming for fine materials such as lawn, organdie, batiste, etc., and are so easily made that it is a pleasure to use the attachment.

Ruffling has long played an important part in trimming garments and the *Ruffler* furnished with the Singer machine will make ruffles of any desired fullness at a speed of ten yards in ten minutes. By a simple adjustment the ruffles can be changed into dainty plaits. This attachment is a wonderful time saver when making trimmings, and it is so simple to use that perfect results may easily be obtained. Photographs illustrating the possibilities of the Ruffler are shown on the opposite page.

The *Quilter* is another useful attachment and enables perfect quilting to be done with the greatest ease. Small pieces of quilting may be used for making up into cushions and for many other decorative purposes. Small articles such as duchesse sets, nightdress cases, are articles suitable for quilted fabrics. For decorative work, the *Underbraider* will be found of the utmost value. Any braid that will fit the underbraider tube and may be stitched through the centre can be used with the attachment.

MAKING CUSHIONS

Cushions form such an important item in the comfort and decoration of a room, that considerable care should be taken that they conform to individual requirements. No article of furniture can add such a distinguishing feature to the colour scheme, or to the sense of comfort, as a well-designed cushion. The essential feature of any cushion should be comfort.

Cushions can be covered with almost any kind of material that will either blend well with existing upholstery or will provide that essential piece of contrast that a successful colour scheme demands.

Plain silks can be embellished with embroidery, pleasing patterns can be arranged in patchwork, suitable material can be woven on a loom; in fact, the possibilities in providing suitable materials are practically unlimited. Cushions provide an excellent way to use quiltings and give scope for putting quilted patterns to good use.

Three different types of cushion are illustrated on the next page. The oblong cushion shown at the top of the page is very easily made in the form of a bag with fringed ends. The filling should be with small feathers or soft down; there are several suitable materials for cushion filling which are quite inexpensive.

The round cushion is suitable for utilising simple embroidery work such as cross stitch and petit-point, for using up beautiful pieces of brocade or tapestry, or for pieces of plain soft silk. The top and bottom are cut to the required diameter and the sides made in one length. Silk cord or a narrow frill will make excellent edgings.

Square cushions are useful for modern furniture and are made similarly to the round cushion. The shape lends itself to piped edges, the piping being made separately and inserted. The square cushion is often made in soft leather, the edges being finished with a piped edge or joined with leather thongs. The filling in a leather cushion can be kept in place by buttons.

OBLONG CUSHION WITH FRINGE

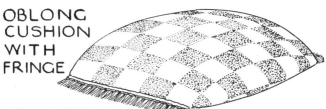

SEW THREE SIDES
INSERT FRINGE IN THE TWO ENDS

ROUND CUSHION EDGED WITH SILK CORD

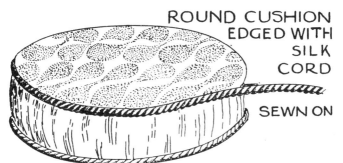

SEWN ON

CUT OUT TWO LARGE CIRCLES
MAKE SEPARATE STRIP FOR SIDES

SQUARE CUSHION

BUTTONS SEWN ON

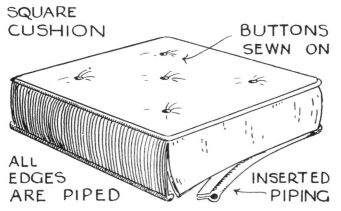

ALL
EDGES
ARE PIPED

INSERTED
PIPING

HOW TO MAKE POUFFES

The particular form of floor cushion known as a pouffe is made in a variety of shapes and sizes. Suggestions are given on the next page for both the square and the round type, but in addition, very useful pouffes can be made from a lidded box with padded surfaces covered with fabric or leather, as shown on page 88.

Pouffes are made similarly to cushions with any suitable fabric. For use in a room furnished with tapestry covered chairs, it is usual to make the case with similar material, but the underside should be made with strong linen or leather in order to withstand the wear.

First of all make a case from canvas, hessian or any fairly strong fabric. Odd pieces from the rag-bag can be joined up in patchwork fashion, because the appearance of the inside case does not matter as long as it is strong. The case can be made to the required depth, but if made in two or more layers, filling will be easier.

Horsehair, especially when fully curled, makes the best filling, but wool, cotton mixture, or torn up rags can be used. There are other materials suitable for stuffing the case such as dried fibre, fine wood shavings. The filling should be distributed carefully inside the case, an upholsterer's needle will be found serviceable. It is advisable to run stitches right through the packing at intervals to prevent it from moving from side to side.

The outer case should be made to fit the inner case as closely as possible. Piped edging is done similarly to that shown on the cushion on page 94. The circular pouffe is finished as a cylinder and tightened up with a cord as indicated.

In planning out the material, as far as possible the top, bottom and the sides should be separate pieces, allowing sufficient for hemming. These portions may, however, be made of several pieces joined together. It is a good plan, when making loose covers, to use up the scrap lengths in making covers for existing or new pouffes.

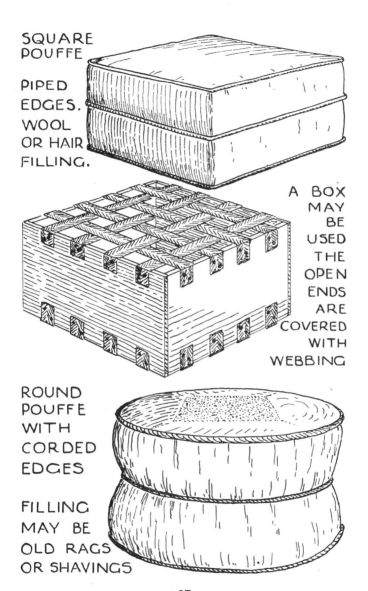

SQUARE
POUFFE

PIPED
EDGES.
WOOL
OR HAIR
FILLING.

A BOX
MAY
BE
USED
THE
OPEN
ENDS
ARE
COVERED
WITH
WEBBING

ROUND
POUFFE
WITH
CORDED
EDGES

FILLING
MAY BE
OLD RAGS
OR SHAVINGS

97

MARKING LINEN

Linen can be marked with a specially prepared ink or with linen and silk thread, the latter being worked directly on the material or on tape. The advantages of ink are rapidity and cheapness, but for good style and serviceableness the thread method is preferable, as, in time, the ink may destroy the fibres, thus causing a hole.

The size of the marking depends on the article and the style mainly on individual taste. As a rule, handkerchiefs are marked at one corner, with either an initial, a monogram or a name. Table napkins are similarly marked. Sheets, pillow-cases and towels are generally marked in the middle of the hemmed end, about 6 in. from the hem to read from the end. Small guest towels are often marked with a monogram in the centre of one half a few inches up from the hem. Tablecloths can be marked on a corner or with a monogram or initial to show on the top of the table about 6 in. from the edge to the right of the hostess.

Some suggestions are given on the next page for suitable embroidered markings. Some thought should be given to the choice of lettering used either for names, initials or monograms. In all cases select a regular place for the marking and adopt a standard form.

The accepted colour for embroideries is usually white ; plain letters, initials and simple monograms can be done quickly in chain, stem or cross stitch. This simple stitch is to be preferred to the more elaborate and raised embroidery for linens which are normally washed by machinery, but for decorative purposes the raised letter is most effective and will last a long time.

The style of lettering decided upon should be drawn out on paper and transferred to the linen with carbon paper. Another method is to use stiff paper, prick holes through at close intervals, use a muslin pounce bag filled with fine resin and then cover with tissue paper and iron with a fairly hot iron.

EMBROIDERED

WOVEN

SIMPLE   MONOGRAMS

EMBROIDERED   SCROLL   INITIALS

DARNING TABLE LINEN AND TOWELS

The housewife who can use a sewing machine can make darns in household napery in a fraction of the time required for hand darning, and the work will be infinitely superior in appearance and will wear and wash better.

The only special fittings required for the work—all of which may be obtained for a small outlay—are a Darning or Embroidery Hoop, a small plate to cover the feed and a little Spring Presser to hold the material in position while the needle is on its upward course.

To ensure a soft smooth finish, it is essential that a fine needle and fine mercerised cotton should be used; these can be obtained from Singer shops. Ordinary cotton results in a rather stiffer and heavier darn.

As the feed of the machine has been covered by the feed cover plate, it will be understood that the movement of the work and the length of the stitch must be controlled by the operator moving the darning hoop. A slow movement of the hand will give a short stitch and a quick movement a longer one. Preliminary practice on a spare piece of material will give confidence.

The hoop should be held with both hands as shown on the next page, and with a steady continuous movement, the work is done backwards and forwards across the hole, keeping the stitches an equal distance apart and running about ¼ in. beyond the edge of the hole and working in the same direction as the weft or fine threads of the material.

After the stitching has been completed one way, turn the hoop round and continue in a similar manner across the first line of stitching. These second lines of stitching should be closer together and run parallel with the warp or thicker threads of the material. Take this stitching about ½ in. beyond the hole, thus covering the first lines of thread entirely. This will strengthen the material without giving a heavy darn.

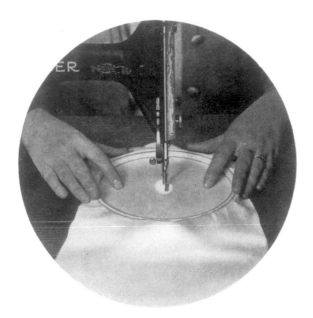

THE SPRING DARNING PRESSER AND NEEDLE
CLAMP WITH THE HOOD AS USED ON A SINGER
SEWING MACHINE.

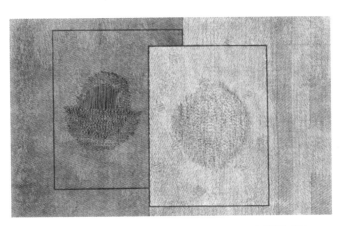

DARNING ON SECTION OF TABLE CLOTH IN
PROCESS AND COMPLETED.

Photograph by "Brillo."

CLEANING POTS AND PANS

Although not always a pleasant job, the cleansing of pots and pans is an important item in culinary duties. In order to reduce the work of cleaning, all cooking utensils should be placed in soak as soon as possible after use. Hot water is essential for greasy utensils and cold water for utensils used for milk and egg dishes.

Equipment for cleaning pots and pans should include soap and fine steel wool, soda and abrasive powder, wooden skewers and newspaper, whiting, oil and metal polish, and suitable cloths for drying.

Aluminium pots and pans are now more commonly used than those made with other metals. Aluminium is slightly affected by acids and alkalis, but not sufficiently so to be injurious. Vegetables will discolour the metal, but acids and fruits brighten and clean it. Do not clean with soda, wash only with pure soap and hot water. Polishing should be done with fine steel wool used with a little soap and hot water and, if a high polish is required, use finely powdered whiting with steel wool; the prepared wool and soap known as Brillo is excellent.

Kitchen utensils made of brass, copper, iron and tin can be washed with hot water and soda to remove grease and rinsed with hot water. Iron pots should be rubbed with an abrasive, using newspaper instead of cloth. Rinse afterwards with hot soap suds, then with clean hot water, and wipe dry while still hot. Tinned saucepans should not be allowed to be in contact with soda for more than a few minutes, they should be rinsed in soapy water, then hot water, and also dried while hot. It should be understood that tinned utensils will not stand continual scouring without gradually wearing out the deposit.

Pewter pots can be cleaned with an abrasive powder, or fine steel wool and oil, washed with soapy and then clean water. Brass and copper utensils are cleaned with metal polish, rinsed and dried warm.

MENDING POTS AND PANS

It is not always necessary to be able to use a soldering bit before a leaky saucepan can be repaired, because small holes can be filled in with pot menders in a perfectly satisfactory manner. In fact while a soldered patch would be ideal for a tin saucepan, it would be difficult to solder a patch on an iron pot, and much more difficult to carry out the same form of repair on aluminium.

Pot menders in several sizes are obtainable at most of the household stores and are very inexpensive ; they consist of two discs of tin, one disc of thin cork, a small screw and nut and a spanner as indicated in the illustration. They are usually supplied on a card, and it is therefore a good plan to keep a card of menders in readiness.

Before the mender is used, the hole should be enlarged if it is smaller than the small screw ; this can be done with the pointed end of an old pair of scissors or with the end of a file and then both surfaces should be scraped quite bright, using an old knife or some emery cloth.

The method of fixing the menders is perfectly simple. First place one of the discs of tin on the screw, then fit the piece of thin cork on top. The projecting end of the screw should be pushed through the hole from the inside of the pot to the outside and held in position with the fingers. Now place the remaining disc of tin over the projecting screw and picking up the small nut, screw it on as tightly as possible with the fingers.

In order to screw up the nut as closely as it is essential that it should be, hold a screwdriver on the bolt from the inside to prevent it turning round, and then place the spanner on the nut on the outside and turn it slowly and gradually until it is difficult to give it another turn.

New handles for a saucepan or kettle lid can be made by using an ordinary bottle cork and driving a wood screw into it from underneath. In the case of small leaks round the spout, it is possible to obtain in tube form, a metallic paste to spread over the leak,

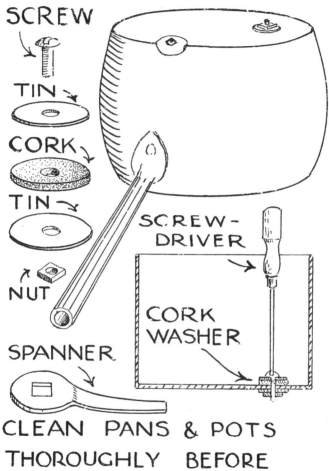

SCREW

TIN

CORK

TIN

NUT

SPANNER

SCREW-
DRIVER

CORK
WASHER

CLEAN PANS & POTS
THOROUGHLY BEFORE
FITTING A POT MENDER

REPAIRING BROKEN CROCKERY

Household crockery in everyday use is usually quite easy to replace and repairs are rarely practicable, especially if the articles have to be washed frequently in hot water. In the case of valuable pieces of china and porcelain, repairs can be carried out with advantage.

To be successful with all forms of crockery repairs, the work should be undertaken as soon as possible after the fracture. If the broken parts are exposed to the air, they are apt to become dusty and the surface will absorb a certain amount of grease from the atmosphere. If arrangements cannot be made at once, all the broken parts should be wrapped carefully in clean paper and kept as air-tight as possible.

Broken plates and ornaments can be repaired with liquid glue or one of the special cements sold for the purpose. The glue should be applied with a brush which should be perfectly clean and the thinnest possible film of glue or cement spread on the fractured places. Avoid touching the broken places with the fingers ; a certain amount of grease cannot be avoided if the fingers are allowed to touch the absorbent pottery.

A considerable amount of pressure should be applied to the cemented join ; this must, of course, be consistent with the strength of the article. A join in a plate can be pulled up very tightly by means of a length of string twisted up with a strip of wood as indicated on the next page. Joins in a vase or similar article are not so easily clamped up. Finger pressure must be applied to work out any excess of glue in the joint and then the article can be bound up with gummed paper tape.

Broken tea-pot and jug handles can be repaired with cement, but in addition it will be necessary to strengthen the join by strips of cane or wire on the inside and, if possible, the outside bend, and then binding the whole together with fine wire or cane. For oven crockery, repairs can be made with specially prepared cement.

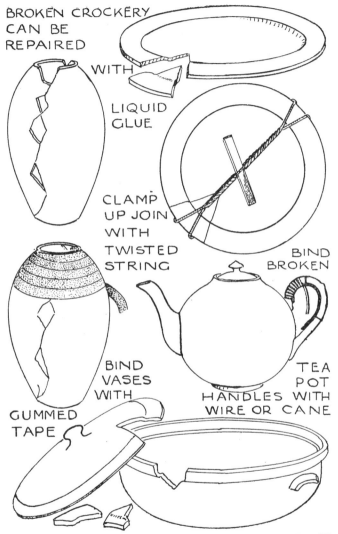

BROKEN CROCKERY CAN BE REPAIRED

WITH

LIQUID GLUE

CLAMP UP JOIN WITH TWISTED STRING

BIND BROKEN

BIND VASES WITH

GUMMED TAPE

TEA POT HANDLES WITH WIRE OR CANE

REPAIR COOKING POTS WITH CEMENT

FIXING TILES AND REPAIRING FIREPLACES

The replacing of a loose tile in the fireplace or on a wall or shelf is a matter for immediate attention. Failure to attend at once to a cracked, broken or loose tile may lead to those surrounding the defective one also becoming loose or damaged.

In modern construction it is usual for tiles to be bedded in a cement formed of equal parts of sand and Portland cement, but in made-up tiled surrounds, a plaster of Paris composition is often used, the latter being softer and much easier to remove than cement.

In any case, the first job is to clean out the space that has been occupied by the tile. In doing this, care must be taken to see that the surrounding tiles are not loose ; if they are, it will be necessary to pull them out as well. If they should still be firmly bedded in, care must be exercised to prevent them being loosened when chipping out any cement or plaster which may adhere to the edges.

A good tool for cleaning out the space is an old table knife cut off short and ground to an edge. A wide screwdriver is also useful. Scrape away all plaster on the edges as well, work out the back to leave a depth at least $\frac{1}{8}$ in., preferably $\frac{1}{4}$ in. more than the thickness of the tile. When the recessing has been completed, clean out with a wet brush, to remove dust and particles and leave the surface in a condition to take the new plaster.

There are cement preparations such as Stixit made up in tube form, which are easily applied and quite effective. Portland cement is readily obtainable ; this can be used neat and mixed with water. To be economical, Portland cement should be mixed with an equal part of fine sand and made into a mortar with water. Do not make cement too wet, just soft enough to move it easily. It can be applied with a knife, but it will be found that a small trowel is more convenient.

Do not place the cement on a dry or smooth surface,

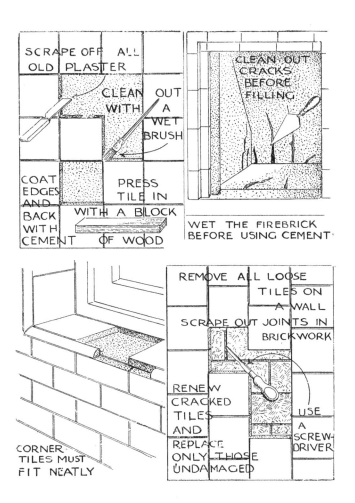

SCRAPE OFF ALL
OLD PLASTER

CLEAN OUT
WITH A
WET
BRUSH

COAT
EDGES
AND
BACK
WITH
CEMENT

PRESS
TILE IN
WITH A BLOCK
OF WOOD

CLEAN OUT
CRACKS
BEFORE
FILLING

WET THE FIREBRICK
BEFORE USING CEMENT·

REMOVE ALL LOOSE
TILES ON
A WALL
SCRAPE OUT JOINTS IN
BRICKWORK

RENEW
CRACKED
TILES
AND
REPLACE
ONLY THOSE
UNDAMAGED

USE
A
SCREW-
DRIVER

CORNER
TILES MUST
FIT NEATLY

this applies particularly to the large surface at the back, and do not apply it too thickly. Before replacing the tile, wet the back and edges and then press into position. It is a good plan to have a short block of wood long enough to overlap the tile and then press firmly from corner to corner until the surplus cement works out.

When the tile has been bedded in, wipe off the cement with a damp cloth and run the point of the trowel or corner of the knife along the join to give a neat finish ; this is known as pointing. Give a final finish to the joint by a light rub with a damp cloth.

Tiles on a wall call for more preparation than those on a hearth and it is advisable to rake out the joints in the brickwork as indicated on the next page. The rougher the surface the better, as it provides a secure hold for the cement. In the case of broken tiles, care must be taken to procure new tiles of the correct size.

When dealing with window sills and recesses as shown (p. 109), the instructions given above will apply, but it will be found that the quarter-round slips require special care. Generally, it is advisable to fit in the flat tiles first and then the corners, but it depends on the position in which the tiles are placed. When dealing with horizontal surfaces, all the tiles can be replaced together, but with vertical tiling much more care must be taken to obtain a strong key for the cement ; with tiles to be placed on a wall previously cemented or plastered, the back is chipped to give a number of deep grooves. Use an old chisel or a screwdriver.

In repairing the firebrick at the back or sides of a fireplace, use a special heat-resisting cement such as Pyruma or Purimachos ; first clean out all the cracks with a fine stiff brush so that fine dust is removed. The special cement should be worked up to a paste and then the cracks should be washed out thoroughly with clean water. The cement should be pressed firmly into the cracks, using a trowel or a small knife, and smoothed off neatly.

FURNITURE POLISHES AND REVIVERS

Considerable care should be exercised in the use of ready prepared furniture polishes and revivers. Surfaces that have been produced by wax or oil well rubbed into the grain can be kept in good condition by any polish having a wax basis, but highly french-polished surfaces and those produced by the application of hard glaze require special treatment.

It should be understood that french polish is produced by a coating of shellac dissolved in spirit and is finally hardened off by spirit alone. Care has to be taken that the polish does not remove the hardened surface; this is easily done if it contains too much spirit.

A temporary brilliancy can be produced by the so-called reviver which actually removes a slight amount of the surface, but if a polish containing a good proportion of wax is not applied at once, the surface will not last very long and is likely to " sweat."

An excellent polish can be made by shredding $1\frac{1}{2}$ oz. of beeswax, $\frac{1}{2}$ oz. white wax, and $\frac{1}{2}$ oz. of castile soap. Place it in a wide-necked jar with $\frac{1}{2}$ pint of turpentine, shake thoroughly until all the wax is dissolved. Now make a lather with white scented soap about the size of an egg with about $\frac{1}{2}$ pint of boiling water, stir the saponified hot water very slowly into the mixture of wax and turpentine and beat it thoroughly to form a cream. This cream when cool should be suitably bottled and used sparingly. It should be applied with a soft rag used with a circular motion and then polished with a soft polishing cloth. In all cases, furniture to be polished should be free from dust and grease, and it is advisable to wipe the polished surfaces first with a wet cloth dipped in warm water in which some pure soap flakes have been dissolved. Apply the polish to a dry surface. The main purpose of a polish is to enrich the surface to which it is to be applied, and in enriching it, a new film is produced.

KEEPING SCISSORS AND KNIVES IN GOOD TRIM

It is by no means a difficult job to keep scissors in first class cutting condition. If the scissors blade are examined, it will be seen that the cutting edges are inclined away from the flat inner faces of the blades. It is these narrow edges that should be kept sharp ; there is no need to sharpen the flat sides at all.

A fine grade of oilstone is a convenience, but the blades can be sharpened almost as well on a piece of finest emery paper, known as Blue back, provided that the paper is glued to a flat strip of wood as shown.

The scissors should be drawn along the paper with the inside of the blade sloping sufficiently to allow the cutting edge to be flat on the hone. The position is shown on a separate diagram ; the blade should be drawn along the hone without altering the inclination of the the blade, with just sufficient pressure to keep the steel in close contact with the abrasive surface.

On further examination of the scissor blades, it will be seen that they are slightly curved towards the tip. The screw pivot should be kept tight enough to allow the whole length of the blades to touch as they are opened and closed. If the pivot should have worked loose, a turn of the screw with a screwdriver should be sufficient.

In the case of scissors that have been well worn, and the screw thread does not tighten up, the remedy is to place the head of the screw on a piece of iron, a flat iron provides a suitable anvil for the purpose, and then tap the end of the screw pivot with a hammer as shown. This method of tightening the blade requires careful hammering, otherwise the blades may be tightened up too much for easy movement.

Knives should be placed almost flat on the hone, pressed down firmly and drawn from one end of the hone to the other ; the main thing is to retain, as far as possible, the original angle.

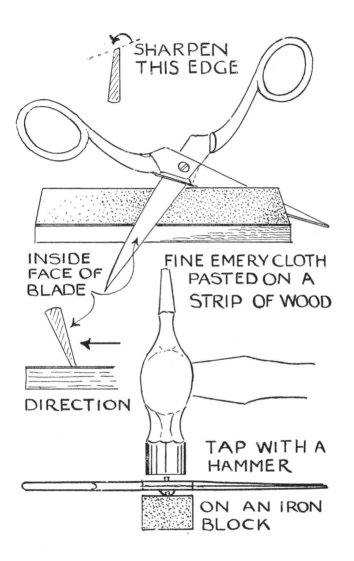

SHARPEN THIS EDGE

INSIDE FACE OF BLADE

DIRECTION

FINE EMERY CLOTH PASTED ON A STRIP OF WOOD

TAP WITH A HAMMER

ON AN IRON BLOCK

FIXING LOOSE KNIFE HANDLES

The handles of table knives are liable to work loose, especially if they are left in hot water ; the cement becomes soft and loses its tenacity. The remedy is to remove the blade, clean the tang as well as the hole and cement the handle on again. Usually, the handle becomes loose enough to be drawn off the tang quite easily, if there should be any difficulty, the blade should be gradually turned until the tang is free.

Some of the old cement will cling to the tang and must be cleaned off with an old knife or a file, the tang should be left as rough as possible. Some care should be taken to remove the cement remaining in the hole in the handle ; a suitable method, shown on the next page, is to use a bradawl as a drill. Keep the tool upright and turn it round, tapping out the old cement from time to time.

There are several forms of paste and liquid cement which may be used, but the difficulty of filling the hole in the handle with anything but a dry powder, renders them inadvisable. By far the simplest method of cementing is to use powdered resin. Provide a small lump of resin, and pound it down in a basin to a fine powder.

The simplest method of introducing the powder into the hole in the handle, is to place it in a small cone-shaped bag with a small hole in the bottom as indicated. As the powder gradually fills up the hole, pack it lightly with a darning or knitting needle to ensure that the hole is completely filled.

Now heat up the tang in a gas flame, not red-hot, but just hot enough to melt the resin. A test can be made by placing the tang in a small pile of powder. Press the tang firmly and quickly into the handle, holding the blade in a cloth, making sure that the handle and blade are in the correct position. The success of cementing depends on having the tang hot enough to melt the resin at the bottom of the hole. Leave the cemented handle for an hour or two before it is moved.

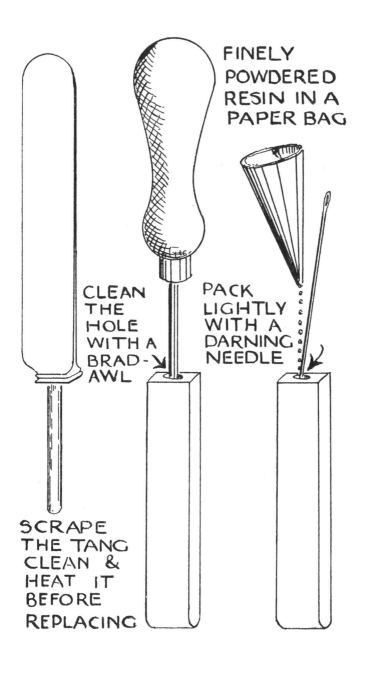

FINELY
POWDERED
RESIN IN A
PAPER BAG

CLEAN
THE
HOLE
WITH A
BRAD-
AWL

PACK
LIGHTLY
WITH A
DARNING
NEEDLE

SCRAPE
THE TANG
CLEAN &
HEAT IT
BEFORE
REPLACING

WHEN THE SINK IS STOPPED UP

Stoppage in the sink is caused usually by an accumulation of grease and small particles of food and grit. The sink should always be flushed out after use with hot soda solution to dissolve the grease and allow a free flow to the outside gulley. It is advisable to give the drainage pipe a good flushing with hot water at least once a day.

If hot water and soda does not clear the pipe, fill up the sink to within a few inches of the top and use a force cup as indicated on the next page. If the force cup fails to exert enough pressure, the cap underneath the U-shaped pipe must be unscrewed and the contents of the pipe run into a bucket. Care must be taken that the contents of the sink is not more than will fill a bucket underneath. It may be necessary to ease out the accumulated refuse with a skewer or a length of wire. When empty, the inside of the pipe should be cleaned out with a wire brush. After replacing the cap, flush out with a strong soda solution. The cap usually has two outside projections and it can be unscrewed by placing a screwdriver held horizontally between them.

The outside gulley is also liable to become clogged, not only at the bottom but also on the inside of the U-bend. Deposits of grease will, if not cleaned off periodically, reduce the size of the opening. The gulley should be flushed out from time to time with a strong solution of soda or a special cleaning compound. In addition, a bent rod as indicated on the next page, should be used to remove deposits at the top of the trap. In hot weather it is advisable to flush all drains with a disinfectant about once a week.

The iron rod suggested for the cleaning of gulleys can be used for clearing clogged W.C. pans. If the stoppage cannot be cleared with the rod, a temporary force cup can be made by wrapping a piece of cloth or old blanket over a mop, tying it securely to the handle.

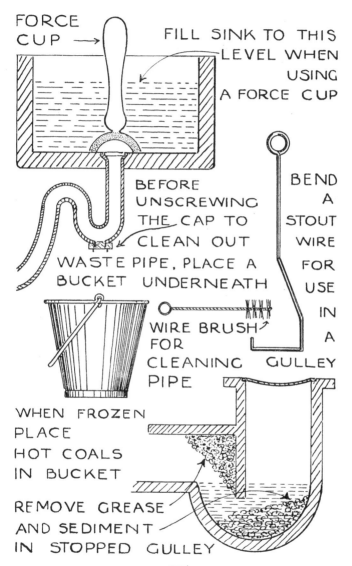

FORCE CUP →

FILL SINK TO THIS LEVEL WHEN USING A FORCE CUP

BEFORE UNSCREWING THE CAP TO CLEAN OUT WASTE PIPE, PLACE A BUCKET UNDERNEATH

BEND A STOUT WIRE FOR USE IN A GULLEY

WIRE BRUSH FOR CLEANING PIPE

WHEN FROZEN PLACE HOT COALS IN BUCKET

REMOVE GREASE AND SEDIMENT IN STOPPED GULLEY

117

REMOVING STAINS

One of the household cupboards should contain preparations for removal of stains and spots. The longer a stain is allowed to remain, the more difficult it becomes to remove. One useful stand-by is Household Ammonia which may be obtained ready for use, or can be made by mixing pure ammonia with an equal quantity of water. An Oxalic Acid solution should also be made: dissolve 1 teaspoonful of oxalic acid crystals in $\frac{3}{4}$ pint of water. Pour into a bottle and label in red letters " POISON."

A bottle of Javelle water is also useful for bleaching. It is made by first dissolving $\frac{1}{2}$ lb. of washing soda in 1 pint of boiling water. Next dissolve $\frac{1}{4}$ lb. of chloride of lime in 1 quart of cold water and then mix the two together and allow to settle. The clear liquid is poured off, bottled and labelled.

Carbon Tetrachloride should also find a place on the shelf as well as a large bottle of detergent; the latter is made by dissolving $1\frac{1}{2}$ oz. of castile soap in 1 pint of hot water, add 3 quarts of cold water and then 4 ozs. of ammonia, 1 oz. alcohol and 1 oz. of ether.

TABLE LINEN. Fruit stains can usually be removed, if treated at once, by placing the stained portion over a large bowl and pouring boiling water over it. If this method is not effective, bleach with oxalic acid and follow with ammonia, afterwards wash. Stubborn spots can usually be removed by first applying a permanganate of potassium solution, as soon as colour changes to brown, apply oxalic acid and finally ammonia. Iron rust, if not too old, can be removed with lemon juice. Old spots should be taken out with oxalic acid, then ammonia and finally soap and water.

CLOTHING. The household detergent given above will be found excellent for use in sponging woollen fabrics. Either a sponge, soft cloth or a brush can be used. After cleaning, wipe over with clean warm water and press when nearly dry. To remove grease spots use ammonia ; if not effective, try carbon tetrachloride applied with a soft clean cloth. Rings may surround the cleaned spot if too much liquid is used.

Many stains such as those caused by sugar, egg, and blood can be removed by cold water alone, and will often disappear after sponging with a detergent. Any stain caused by a greasy substance, including milk, cream, ice cream, gravy, and liquids containing milk should be taken out with carbon tetrachloride.

Ink spots should not be rubbed ; apply a damp cloth at once so that the ink is absorbed. Stubborn spots should be treated with oxalic acid, the latter being dropped exactly on the spot, absorbed with a cloth, and when the spot has disappeared treat with ammonia. Grass stains can be removed with Fullers Earth or glycerine, and wiped with a damp cloth or washed.

MILDEW. This is caused by allowing clothes to remain damp in a warm place or through clothing being kept in a damp cupboard or chest. The stain can be removed with Javelle water or oxalic acid followed by ammonia. The formation of mildew is preventable and does not occur with dry clothing.

CARPET AND FLOOR STAINS. For carpets, use one of the methods described above according to the particular kind of stain. Ink stains on the floor or on unvarnished wood can be taken out with oxalic acid followed by ammonia to neutralise the acid. Ink stains on polished wood are more difficult to remove. If they cannot be wiped off with plain water, either oxalic acid or spirit must be used, but these fluids will also remove some of the polish. In the latter case, the cleaned place should be re-polished.

PAINT AND VARNISH. Ordinary paint and varnish spots can be removed with turpentine, those made with cellulose paints should be treated with amyl acetate. Delicate materials such as silk should be lightly rubbed with carbon tetrachloride.

PREPARING FLOORS FOR STAINING

It is much more trouble, as a rule, to prepare a floor for staining than to apply the stain, but it is so important that the job must neither be neglected or hurried if a lasting finish is desired.

Projecting nails should be hammered down, and although not essential, the heads of the nails should be driven below the surface with a nail punch. This is particularly important when dealing with old floors.

Rough places, also caused by wear or bad planing should be smoothed; the simplest and most effective tool is a hook scraper as shown in the diagram. The same tool can be used to level the edges of boards that have curled up. It is inexpensive and has a variety of uses in the home.

Small holes caused by nails, places where the knots have dropped out, unsightly gaps between boards and any mouse holes should be filled with plastic wood, or filled with a plastic mixture made with glue and powdered whiting. This material may be stained by mixing some of the stain with it.

Finally the floor should be scrubbed thoroughly and rinsed quite clean. Allow the floor to dry and then rub it over with glasspaper to leave the wood as smooth as possible. Before any stain is applied the floor should be swept free from dust and must be perfectly dry.

If a stained surround only is required, carry out the above operations only on the portions to be stained, but if the remainder of the floor is to be covered with either carpet or linoleum, it is always advisable to make quite sure that there are no projecting nails or large holes, otherwise the floor covering will get damaged.

Floors that have been previously stained should be washed. As far as possible the old coating of stain should be removed, either by scraping or by the application of strong soda or sugar soap. After using either solvent the floor should be rinsed clean.

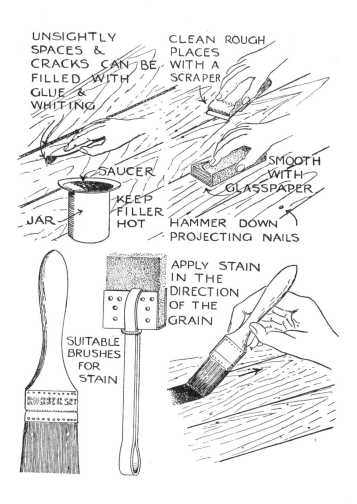

UNSIGHTLY SPACES & CRACKS CAN BE FILLED WITH GLUE & WHITING

CLEAN ROUGH PLACES WITH A SCRAPER

SAUCER

JAR

KEEP FILLER HOT

SMOOTH WITH GLASSPAPER

HAMMER DOWN PROJECTING NAILS

SUITABLE BRUSHES FOR STAIN

APPLY STAIN IN THE DIRECTION OF THE GRAIN

RUBBER SET

STAINING AND POLISHING FLOORS

Before staining is done, the floor should have been prepared as suggested on page 120, and be quite dry and clean. There are two methods of treatment, one is to use a stain first and then to polish with prepared wax, the other is to combine the two operations and use an oil varnish stain such as Varnene.

With ordinary staining, care should be taken to provide a stain of good quality. It is possible to stain new floors quite effectively with a strong solution of permanganate of potash. One of the most effective stains for floors, as well as other woodwork, is Colron; it is a wood dye with considerable penetrating power, and is available in a number of pleasing shades.

The stain can be applied with a special felt brush or with an ordinary bristle brush as indicated. The liquid should be applied in the direction of the grain and brushed on evenly, allowing the dye to work well into the grain. Do not try and make the stain cover as much ground as possible, but apply just enough to soak into the wood.

When the stain has had time to dry thoroughly, one of the well known wax floor polishes can be applied, the method being to use a generous amount of wax and rub it well into the grain with a hard brush. Too much trouble cannot be taken to apply a good coating of wax. Leave the floor for a day or two before the final polishing is done with a soft cloth or a special floor polisher.

An oil varnish stain is easily applied; work in the direction of the grain as shown in the photograph, using as wide a brush as possible. In order to prevent loose fibres, the brush should be of good quality and rubber-set. This particular stain does not dry rapidly like a combined spirit stain and varnish; it is much more effective and gives a lasting surface. Oil varnish stain is equally suitable for furniture.

OIL VARNISH STAIN IS SIMPLE TO APPLY AND
IMPARTS A BEAUTIFUL FINISH TO A FLOOR.

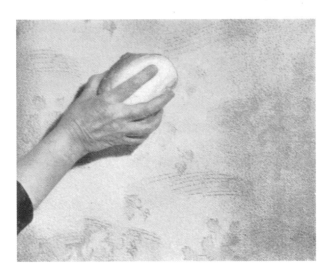

CLEANING WALLPAPER WITH STALE BREAD.

REPAIRING TEARS IN WALLPAPER WITH PASTE.

CLEANING AND REPAIRING WALLPAPER

Walls covered with paper require dusting even more than those finished with distemper or paint. A soft brush is more useful than a cloth, and, if fitted with a long handle, the whole of a wall can be dusted with ease.

Dust marks that have been rubbed into the surface of the paper can be cleaned off with one of the gum or paste cleaners supplied for the purpose, but a ready means, shown on the opposite page, is to use stale bread. Rub lightly, but firmly, until the bread crumbles away.

Finger marks are usually difficult to remove, as are any other form of grease deposited on the surface. A useful method which will remove most grease spots is to soak a piece of lint or absorbent cotton in some grease solvent, such as alcohol or carbon tetrachloride. Apply the wet pad to the place and press firmly ; this process must be repeated until the grease is absorbed by the pad ; a good many applications will be needed to obtain a successful result. Small spots of grease can often be removed by covering them with two or three thicknesses of blotting paper and placing a hot iron on top. The iron must not be hot enough to scorch the paper, just sufficiently hot to melt grease.

Tears in wallpaper require careful treatment. First lift up the torn portion and smooth it out, being careful not to damage the edges in any way. Mix up some flour paste or make a paste with prepared powder and place in a basin or jar in a convenient position. Cover a book or piece of board with clean wrapping paper and press the torn portion over as indicated.

Apply the paste to the back of the torn strip as shown ; do not attempt to apply any paste to the wall. Allow a few minutes for the paste to moisten the paper and then press carefully in position. If a rubber roller is available, press the paper down, if not, cover with clean blotting paper and smooth down, working to the point of the tear.

CLEANING DISTEMPERED WALLS

There are several ways of cleaning distemper, or water paint as it is sometimes called; these depend on the kind of distemper used and the condition of the surface. Walls discoloured by damp or by the lime in the cement or in the plaster coating can only be treated by washing off the old coat and applying new distemper. Grease marks must be removed by a solvent before any further treatment of the surface can be undertaken.

If the walls have been treated with a washable distemper, clean water applied with a sponge will brighten up the surface, but the sponge and the water must be kept clean. It is, however, a better plan to try the effect of a brush first. Use a good quality boot brush with stiff bristles and work with a circular motion from the top of the wall downwards. The dry brush will remove a certain amount of fine powder, but usually it will leave the wall clean.

Thick grease spots should be scraped off and then the mark cleaned with a rag soaked in carbon ultra-chloride, petrol, gasolene or strong soda. In any case it will be difficult to take out any grease mark by scraping without removing some of the distemper underneath. Greasy finger marks however can often be removed from a distempered wall by first covering the place with clean blotting paper and pressing a hot iron over it. After the grease has been removed, the wall should be lightly brushed over with a hard dry brush.

As it is difficult to avoid marks on a distempered wall and also difficult to match the exact tint, it is always advisable to retain a small quantity of the original wash in a tightly stoppered bottled, or air-tight tin, so that damaged places may be covered with new distemper. Use a stiff paint brush, a stencil brush is ideal, spread some of the distemper on a piece of board, fill in the damaged portion thickly and then stipple the edges so that the wash is gradually merged into the main surface.

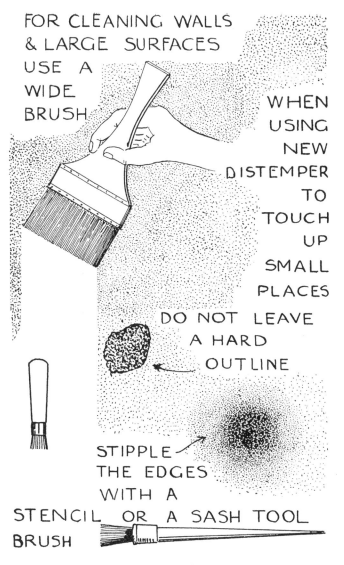

FOR CLEANING WALLS
& LARGE SURFACES
USE A
WIDE
BRUSH

WHEN
USING
NEW
DISTEMPER
TO
TOUCH
UP
SMALL
PLACES

DO NOT LEAVE
A HARD
OUTLINE

STIPPLE
THE EDGES
WITH A
STENCIL OR A SASH TOOL
BRUSH

CLEANING PAINT WORK

All painted surfaces seem to have a special attraction for dust and grease from the atmosphere, especially in foggy weather, and if this film of grease and dust is allowed to remain on the paint, the oxidising and discolouring acids contained in it will gradually penetrate and cause discoloration. The remedy is frequent washing with pure soap suds, and warm water. Strong soaps containing soda should not be used.

Although in the pure air of the country, paint will retain its freshness for a long time, the contaminated air of the town areas, especially where there are many factories, will cause painted surfaces to deteriorate in a few months. This is likely to happen with even the best qualities of paint, but with careful treatment it will retain its freshness for a long time.

Cleaning paint does not mean hard rubbing ; generally all that is necessary is to make a lather of pure soap flakes, apply it with a sponge, and then wash the soapy water with a clean sponge, finally drying with a cloth.

For paint work in kitchens, where more than the ordinary amount of grease is likely to be deposited, it is advisable to use a solvent, such as sugar soap or soda, but it should be used sparingly and rinsed off with tepid water directly the paint is clean. Polish with a dry cloth.

The gloss on a highly enamelled surface, particularly in the case of an oil enamel, may lose its brilliancy after cleaning. The remedy in this case is to polish the surface with a soft chamois leather. With dark shades, use a few drops of linseed oil, but with pale tints, such as white and cream, use a little olive oil. Soak a small pad of cotton wool with the oil, wrap the pad inside a piece of soft linen or cambric (an old handkerchief is excellent), rub very lightly over the surface and then polish vigorously, but lightly, with the leather. Any painted surface which, after successive cleaning, loses its gloss, will be improved by a coat of clear varnish.

WASH PAINT
WITH A
SPONGE

CLEAN OUT
MOULDINGS

WITH AN OLD
TOOTHBRUSH

USE SOAP FLAKES MADE
INTO A LATHER
REMOVE GREASE SPOTS
WITH A SODA SOLUTION

EASING DOORS AND DRAWERS

The failure of a door to open easily, a drawer to run smoothly or a window sash to open readily, may be due to several reasons, but usually the stickiness is caused either by some portion of the woodwork having swollen ; or another part may be warped or shrunk or because of an excess of paint. Generally, the trouble can be cured by the use of a scraper.

A suitable form of scraper comprises a steel hook set in a wooden handle, the Skarsten being a typical type. This scraper is easily handled and should form an item in the household equipment ; it can be used for smoothing floorboards, and for removing thick deposits of paint.

To deal with a sticky door, first note the points where the door sticks. With a painted door a few strokes of the scraper may remove the excess, but rather than remove all the paint from the edge of the door, it is better to take a little off the door and the jamb. In the case of a door which drags on the floor, it is possible to effect a cure by extending the hook of the scraper and remove a few shavings, but if the door has dropped considerably, the better plan is to have the door taken down and the bottom edge planed off.

The lower portion of the sides of a drawer can be scraped to reduce the width, but care should be taken to see if the trouble is not caused by the runners inside the framework or carcase. Examine the inside of the drawer opening and note the condition of the strips of wood which are intended to allow the drawer to run easily. They may have worked loose ; if screwed, the screws should be tightened. If the runners have been glued in position, they should be cleaned and re-glued or screwed.

Sticky window sashes are often caused by an excess of paint on the beading. A few strokes of the scraper will usually be sufficient ; care should be taken to scrape only the inside edges of the beading and only at the points where the sash appears to bind.

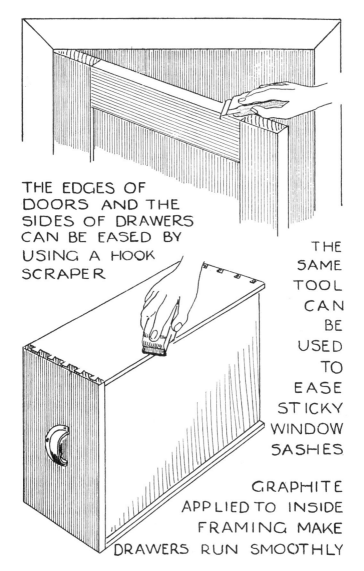

THE EDGES OF
DOORS AND THE
SIDES OF DRAWERS
CAN BE EASED BY
USING A HOOK
SCRAPER

THE
SAME
TOOL
CAN
BE
USED
TO
EASE
STICKY
WINDOW
SASHES

GRAPHITE
APPLIED TO INSIDE
FRAMING MAKE
DRAWERS RUN SMOOTHLY

RE-POLISHING WITH SHELLAC

Although all the best work must be polished by hand, much of the preliminary bodying may be done with shellac varnish, applied with a brush. French polishing, once a lengthy operation, has now been superseded to a great degree by hard gloss which gives a highly glossed surface, but it is susceptible to stains and heat marks.

The methods to be employed in removing stains and marks on polished surfaces are described on page 145, and usually it is necessary to re-polish the renovated surface. It is often difficult to touch up small places with varnish without showing the newly varnished edges, which in some cases may be rather displeasing.

Presuming that the best possible finish is desired, the most suitable treatment is french polish, that is shellac dissolved in methylated or denatured spirit similarly to the varnish, but instead of being brushed on it is applied with a pad. In this way portions of a surface can be re-polished without a visible edge.

The polish can be obtained ready for use ; it is used by applying a few drops to a pad of cotton wool as shown, the moistened pad being covered with a fine linen rag, folded as indicated. Rub the pad lightly with a continuous circular motion, moistening the wool with fresh polish as it is worked out. A touch or so of linseed oil on the surface of the pad from time to time will ease the rubbing. When sufficiently polished, the polish inside the pad should be replaced gradually with pure spirit in order to harden the surface. The surface of the pad will need a touch of oil to prevent it sticking.

French polishing should be done in a warm room in stages rather than at one sitting. If two or three separate films of polish are rubbed on at intervals of a day or so, the result will be much more satisfactory. The most delicate part of the work lies in the finishing ; if too much spirit is used, all the previous polish may be removed instead of existing polish being hardened.

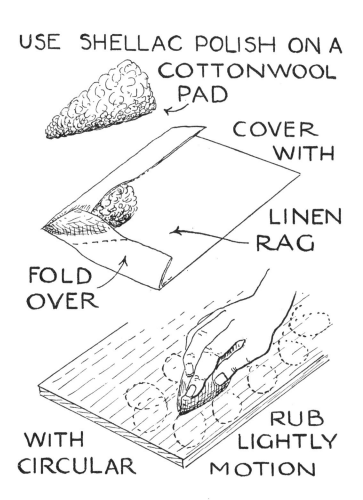

USE SHELLAC POLISH ON A COTTONWOOL PAD

COVER WITH LINEN RAG

FOLD OVER

WITH CIRCULAR RUB LIGHTLY MOTION

FINISH POLISHING WITH A LITTLE SPIRIT ON THE PAD

USING PAINT AND ENAMEL

There are many kinds of paint which may be easily applied by the housewife. But before any form of paint is used, the surface to which it is to be applied must be clean and, generally, it should be smooth. Too much trouble cannot be taken to prepare the surface ; this is not only to make the actual painting easier, but to economise the material.

Full instructions are given on page 128, for cleaning paint ; these instructions should be followed, but it should be noted that, as a rule, it is better to remove the old paint before a new coat is applied. It is not always necessary, except in the case of exterior paint work, to clean down the surface to the bare wood, but to remove the top film and leave the surface smooth. Glasspaper or pumice powder applied with a felt pad will generally be sufficient.

It is always economical to use paint of the best quality, it lasts longer and has a greater covering capacity. A good brush is essential; those set in rubber are best.

In applying paint, work downwards from top to bottom, pick up just sufficient paint to fill the brush and spread the paint evenly. Ordinary oil paint should be thoroughly worked, but enamels can be allowed to flow over the surface. In painting portions of a surface, the edges of the fresh paint should be merged into the old paint by stippling the edges with a dry brush.

Cracks and small holes can be filled in with plastic wood and rubbed down when hard with glasspaper. Usually it is a good plan to apply two coats of paint ; the first one is allowed to dry and is then rubbed down smooth with glasspaper or pumice.

Oil paints are those in which the pigment is suspended in a mixture of linseed oil and turpentine. Enamel paints are, as a rule, mixed with varnish. Lacquer and cellulose paints require special care : they dry rapidly and with a hard and generally a glossy surface.

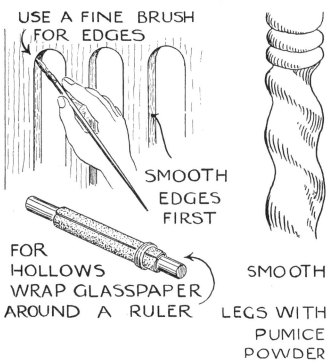

USE A FINE BRUSH
FOR EDGES

SMOOTH
EDGES
FIRST

FOR
HOLLOWS
WRAP GLASSPAPER
AROUND A RULER

SMOOTH
LEGS WITH
PUMICE
POWDER

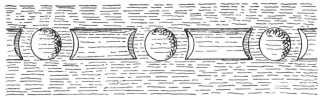

CLEAN OUT MOULDING WITH
FINE PUMICE POWDER
USE A STENCIL OR A TOOTHBRUSH

MATCHING AND PATCHING LINOLEUM

Given proper attention, even the cheapest qualities of linoleum can be made to last a considerable time. Inlaid qualities, used either as a surround or as a complete floor covering, are practically everlasting, but worn places may occur under heavy chairs or tables, or an overlooked projecting nail underneath, or holes may result from a cinder from the fire.

In the event of a portion of the lino being damaged, a little care in patching and in matching the pattern will effect an unnoticeable repair. A suggestion is given on the next page for a patch on a piece of lino with a parquet design. The method with an inlaid pattern: to cut out the damaged portion follow the lines of the pattern as indicated in the lower corner by the thick lines. A new piece is placed underneath, marked out with chalk and then cut accurately to fit.

It is a good plan when cutting lino, especially if the edges of a pattern cannot be followed, to cut through the upper damaged layer as well as the new piece underneath, the latter being so placed that the pattern coincides. It is advisable, in this case, to drive a few brads through both layers so that the underpiece will not move while it is being cut. The brads can be pulled out afterwards with pincers. The best tool for the purpose is a specially shaped lino knife, but it is essential that the cutting edges should be kept as keen as possible. A good hone may be made by pasting a strip of fine emery cloth on a strip of wood. In use, draw the edge of the knife backwards and forwards, press firmly, but keep the blade nearly flat.

Lino can be attached to the floor with cement, but, as a rule, it will be found more convenient to use the special brads or sprigs which are made for the purpose. The brads should be driven in quite straight with the heads flush with the surface. Linoleum attached in this way can be removed easily.

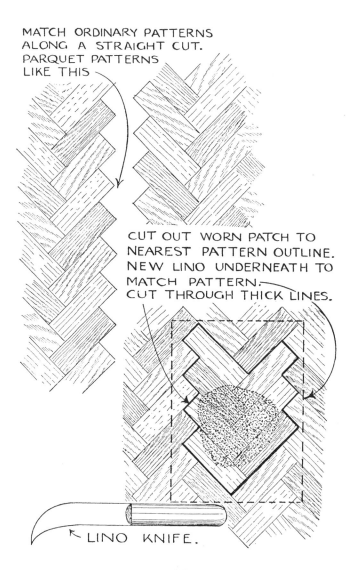

MATCH ORDINARY PATTERNS
ALONG A STRAIGHT CUT.
PARQUET PATTERNS
LIKE THIS

CUT OUT WORN PATCH TO
NEAREST PATTERN OUTLINE.
NEW LINO UNDERNEATH TO
MATCH PATTERN.
CUT THROUGH THICK LINES.

← LINO KNIFE.

137

REPAIRING AND BINDING CARPETS

Minor repairs to carpets, such as frayed edges, can be carried out with little difficulty, but the replacing of portions actually worn out or caused by burns is not easy. Providing that the damaged portion is not more than two or three inches in area, new threads or tufts can usually be matched; if the back of the fabric has been destroyed, a piece of hessian or coarse canvas should be sewn on underneath. With Wilton and Axminster patterns, the tufts are sewn into the back and trimmed off with scissors on a level with the existing pile.

In the case of carpets that are worn in places at considerable distances apart, the best treatment, especially when they are made up with strips, is to take the seams apart and remake the carpet with the least worn portions replacing those showing the most wear. Usually it is easier to cut up the carpet and make it up as a number of rugs, the edges being bound with a blanket stitch or with braid.

Suggestions are given on the next page for the use of the blanket stitch for the cut edges of a pile carpet. In the case of closely woven carpets the stitch can be worked between every three or four tufts, but with a loosely woven Indian carpet, the stitches should be carried well into the edge at close intervals. The latter type of carpet does not lend itself to a braided edge, but braid can be used with advantage on Brussels, Wilton and Axminster carpets.

It rarely happens that a carpet wears out entirely; there are usually portions that have been protected by tables, chairs and other pieces of furniture and remain in good condition. These portions should be cut out, the edges bound, and used for bedside strips or for door slips, for car mats and other useful purposes. Odd pieces of pile carpets covered at the back with leather or leather cloth make excellent foot muffs.

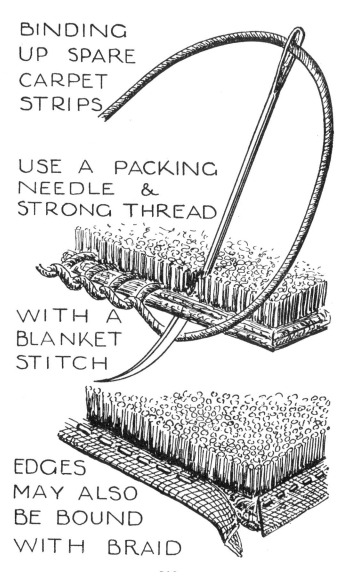

BINDING
UP SPARE
CARPET
STRIPS

USE A PACKING
NEEDLE &
STRONG THREAD

WITH A
BLANKET
STITCH

EDGES
MAY ALSO
BE BOUND
WITH BRAID

139

KEEPING THE GAS STOVE IN GOOD CONDITION

Economy in time and labour can be saved by daily attention to the gas stove. As soon as possible after the stove has been in use and while it is still warm, any spilled liquid or food, or spatterings of grease should be wiped off with a crushed newspaper. Rub over again with a clean piece of paper and the stove will be clean.

If spilled liquid, especially if of a syrupy nature, is allowed to remain on the inside of the oven or on the grids, it will harden, and if the oven is heated again will carbonise. If rubbing with newspaper does not remove the deposit, use soapy water and fine steel wool or a metal mop, and dry with clean newspaper.

A moist cloth should be used to wipe over the stove completely once a week ; if the metal is not enamelled, mix equal quantities of paraffin and turpentine for use in moistening the cleaning cloth and give a final polish with crushed newspaper.

Burners for the stove should be detached and cleaned periodically. The simplest way of cleaning them is to place them in a large bowl and cover them with a hot soda solution, about ½ lb. of soda to a gallon of water. If the burners have been neglected, the bowl should be placed under a gas ring and the water brought to the boil. If the small holes in the burners are clogged with a carbon deposit, clean them out with a piece of wire or a pipe cleaner. Usually, a light scrub with a brush will be sufficient to remove grease, but in the case of difficulty steel wool or a wire brush can be used.

Always dry the burners after cleaning and wipe them over with the paraffin and turpentine solution afterwards. In replacing the burners, examine the supply nozzle, cleaning it out if necessary with some fine wire, taking care not to enlarge the orifice. The tray under the top burners as well as the drip tray at the bottom of the oven should be wiped clean every day.

CLEAN GAS BURNERS IN HOT WATER AND SODA
WITH A STIFF BRUSH.

CLOGGED HOLES CAN BE CLEARED WITH WIRE.

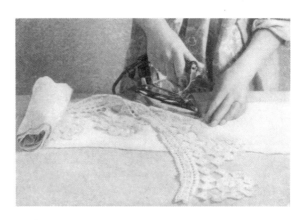

IRONING SHOULD BE DONE AT A CONVENIENT
HEIGHT.

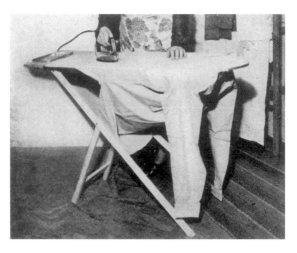

FOLDING IRONING BOARDS ARE GENERALLY
MORE CONVENIENT THAN A TABLE.

ELECTRIC IRONS AND IRONING

The electric iron is one of the most popular of labour-saving devices and, properly used, has an exceedingly long life. There are many different patterns, the most modern types have switches giving various degrees of heat with thermostatic control. Hand irons are attached to a convenient heating plug by a flexible cord.

Ironing boards are an important part of the equipment for successful ironing. Boards should be about 54 in. long, and not less than 12 in. wide, one end being rounded off. Although an ironing board can be supported on two chairs, it is more convenient to use one with a folding support so that it can be placed near a good light and also within reach of a wall plug. The board should be padded to give a firm, but not cushiony, surface. A sleeve board is a labour saver, but the ironing surface should be firmly padded.

It is rarely that the heating element inside the iron fails to function, but care should be taken to avoid using it for long periods at its maximum heating capacity. With a thermostat, any risk of over-heating is avoided ; with an ordinary iron, the current should be turned off from time to time. Irons left unattended with the current on are a frequent cause of fire. When not in use, the electric iron should be kept on its special rack and turned off at once.

Mention has been made on another page of the necessity to hold the plug and not the cord in disconnecting the iron. This applies also to the adaptor which fits on the pins projecting from the iron. In case the adaptor becomes loose, insert a knife or fine screwdriver in the slot so that the ends of the pins are opened slightly. Information will be found on page 74, regarding the method of renewing the cord connections in case they are broken. In the course of time, the rubber insulation is liable to perish, especially if it is allowed to get hot by being left in front of a fire.

CLEANING CARPETS

Accumulations of dust and dirt are the chief causes of discoloration and dinginess in carpets and these are not entirely removed by brushing. The regular use of a vacuum cleaner throughout the year is the best preservative for a carpet, especially those with a thick pile such as Indian carpets. The vacuum cleaner will not, however, remove stains and grease, and it is necessary, therefore, to use special means to remove them.

In large towns it is impossible to keep carpets free from even slight greasy deposits caused through atmospheric conditions, and in order to remove them the carpet should be washed over during the spring cleaning with a good carpet soap, or a solution of ox-gall in the proportion of $\frac{1}{4}$ pint of ox-gall to 2 pints of warm water.

The best way of tackling the actual washing is to have ready one pail of hot water, another of tepid water, a large sponge, a small hard scrubbing brush with long fibres, a flour dredger filled with borax, some carpet soap, and some large dry cloths. First wring the sponge out in the hot water and wash over as large a portion as can be easily reached. Sprinkle the damp patch with the dry borax and then dip the brush into the hot water, rub some soap on the brush and then work it into a lather on the carpet. As soon as the lather is discoloured, dip the sponge in the hot water, squeeze it dry and then lift up the lather. Repeat the lathering with the soap only if necessary, and when the carpet appears to be quite clean, dip the sponge in the tepid water, squeeze most of the water out and wipe over until all traces of lather have been taken off.

If the carpet has faded through the bleaching action of the sun it is not possible entirely to revive the original colouring, but the colours can be brightened if the water used in the final rinsing, (that is after the lather has been washed off), has vinegar mixed with it. A suitable proportion is a teacupful of vinegar to one gallon of water.

REMOVING MARKS ON POLISHED
SURFACES

Marks on highly polished surfaces may be caused by accident or through bad workmanship. French polish applied to a surface insufficiently prepared will develop a minutely pitted surface or become streaky. If subjected to damp, the surface will develop a bloom and even show signs of peeling or cracking. Any surface not regularly treated with a polish will deteriorate.

If the surface of the polish is marred by white marks caused by the action of hot plates or dishes or by damp caused by a porous flower pot, for example, ordinary furniture polish generally will have little or no effect. One remedy is to rub the discoloured place with a soft rag moistened with olive oil and continue until the marks disappear. Rub the place afterwards with a dry cloth, leave for some hours, then use a good furniture polish.

If the surface is badly damaged and the above treatment will not answer, it will be necessary to use a little fine pumice powder with the oil and to rub lightly until the marks are worked out. Finishing in this case should be carried out with french polish as advised on page 132. Actually, this is the only satisfactory method of dealing with scorch marks which have penetrated into the polish.

Scratches that have removed some of the polish and have cut into the surface require careful treatment: a small area surrounding the scratch should be rubbed down with pumice powder and oil to remove the top film of polish. The scratch should be worked out if not too deep, but if it will not disappear, fill it up with pure polish, rub it down smooth and then repolish as above. If the scratches are only slight, a camel hair brush dipped in polish will be sufficient to obliterate them.

Dents may be raised by the application of a hot iron after moistening with water ; effective on plain wood, the greatest care must be taken to avoid damaging a polished surface more than is necessary.

WASHING FABRICS

Before beginning to wash the household linen and soiled clothing, separate the coloured from the white materials, and the silks from the woollens. Look over for torn or damaged parts, and if inconvenient to make the necessary repairs at once, at least tack them up to prevent further damage. Note stains and grease marks and remove them.

White linen and cottons should be placed in cold water to soak, and greasy and very soiled clothing should be rubbed with soap and placed separately in warm water. Usually, it will be sufficient to add a small quantity of soap flakes or soap solution to the water used for soaking. Economy of work, time and materials is the result of soaking clothes before washing.

As far as possible, each article should be washed clean before being placed in the boiler; it is also advisable to rinse the articles prior to placing in the boiler. It is better to soak the fine white things such as table linen, the bed and body linen separately, and then the coarse things such as towels, dusters, overalls, etc.

Boiling should not be done in water unless it contains sufficient soap to maintain a continual lather; too little soap in the water will cause a scum. Small articles such as handkerchiefs are more conveniently handled if placed in a bag. Long boiling, as a rule, is not necessary, from 5 to 20 minutes, an average is about 10 minutes. While the articles are being boiled they should be pressed down into the suds and stirred gently.

After boiling, articles should be rinsed twice in hot water and finally in cold water. If the articles are to be blued, add the blue to cold water to the colour desired. It is better to prepare a separate bath for blueing rather than add the blue to the last rinsing water still containing the clothes. When in the blueing water, keep the articles stirred, lift up large articles to ensure that the blue is distributed evenly. Blue is also helpful in restoring whiteness to both silks and woollies.

Drying washed clothes is as important as the actual washing and care should be taken in wringing out the rinsing water not to injure the materials. A rubber wringer is almost an essential, but it must always be kept scrupulously clean. Out-door drying is to be preferred, but in smoky towns it is often disastrous. Drying in front of a fire is not desirable, the better method, if the clothes cannot be placed out of doors, is to hang them in a room with open windows and doors. Clothes should always be dried as soon as possible after washing ; never leave damp clothes about. If they have to be passed through a mangle or ironed, they should be thoroughly dried first and then damped a short time before ironing.

WOOLLENS, including mixtures, should neither be soaked or boiled, and should be washed without rubbing or friction. The water for washing should be prepared with soap flakes thoroughly worked into a lather ; free soap is liable to cling to the articles. Work out the dirt by squeezing, and if the suds become very dirty, mix up another lot rather than finish in the dirty water. If the water should be hard, soften it with a little household ammonia or some powdered borax.

Careful rinsing is important when washing woollens ; use lukewarm water and rinse several times to ensure that all soap has been eliminated. Ordinary wringing should not be resorted to : place the articles in a towel or cloth and press out the surplus water. If passed through a wringer, wrap up the articles first.

Quick drying is essential. Stretch out and as far as possible dry flat. An ideal method of drying is to stretch a piece of netting in a suitable place outside and place the articles to dry some distance above the ground. If woollen articles must be hung up through lack of convenience to dry them flat, special care must be exercised to prevent them getting out of shape. Clothes hangers will be found useful; in any case, as much of the article should be supported and reliance should not be placed on one or two pegs. Woollens need not be quite dry before ironing if this is necessary, but they should not remain damp any longer than necessary.

SILKS and artificial fabrics are treated similarly to woollens, but special care must be taken to use only the purest soap flakes. Strong washing flakes or soap powders should not on any account be used, particularly those containing soda. Particular care is needed for artificial silks and other fabrics, because the fibres are weakened by moisture. Hot water should not be used, rinsing should be carefully done and care taken in drying. It is only when artificial silks are dry that they are strong enough to be handled other than delicately.

COLOURED MATERIALS. Unless it is known that the colours of fabrics to be washed are fast, it is always advisable to test a small corner if a scrap piece of the material is not available. Usually, colours will not run or fade if the water used is lukewarm only, and the soap is pure. Usually, if the colour of any material does run, it can be traced to the presence of soda in the washing water. It is inadvisable to rub coloured articles when washing; squeezing and pressing should be sufficient. The rinsing waters should be cool and the articles run through the wringer as gently as possible.

BLANKETS. If it is desired to wash blankets at home, treat as for woollens, but it should be noted that unless they are dried quickly in a good breeze, they are likely to felt and shrink. The water should be soft; the ideal is to use clean rain water and to wash one at a time if single-handed.

KNITTED GARMENTS. Knitted and crochetted garments are more liable than any other form of woollen to shrink, or at least to become misshapen. Wash as for woollen articles, but the greatest care is needed in pressing out the rinsing water. Always pull the garment into shape before drying and place flat on a clean cloth.

SIMPLE DRY CLEANING

It is not always convenient to send to the cleaners soiled articles made from fabrics not suitable for washing, and in these days when petrol or gasolene is available, almost at every street corner, full use should be made of the spirit. The utmost care should be taken when using volatile liquids ; work in the open air, if not in a room with any bare lights extinguished and no open fire.

It is much better to dip the material to be cleaned in a receptacle and cover with spirit, stirring it well so that every part is able to absorb it. Failing a sufficient quantity, it can be applied to the material with a soft cloth or a brush. Before placing in the spirit or using it on the surface, the material should be freed from dust, and it is a good plan to wipe or brush soiled places with cold water first. Rubber gloves are advisable if the hands are likely to come into contact with spirit.

A useful form of dry cleaning, especially suitable for felt hats and smooth fabrics, is " Fullers Earth." It is the main component of " cloth balls." Actually it is a dried clay, composed mainly of silica and alumina ; its action is to absorb grease and oil.

In use the Fullers Earth is made into a thick paste with clean water and is spread on the fabric entirely to cover the soiled portion. It is allowed to dry and then it is brushed off with a fairly stiff brush. As far as possible the brushing should be done out of doors in a breeze, so that the dust is blown away. Fullers Earth is inexpensive and can be used for cleaning mats and carpets ; in this case the brushing should be done with a vacuum cleaner if inconvenient to work out of doors.

There is a convenient hand cleaner composed of a brush and a container for a cleansing fluid. One well-known make is the Mutax. It will be found very useful on a holiday to remove stains and spots. There are also various cleansing fluids and pastes packed in convenient forms which can be used for the same purpose.

CLEANING GLOVES

Glove cleaning at home means not only a saving in expense but also in wear. Gloves should not be allowed to get too soiled because the rubbing required to remove dirty marks tends to make the leather thin, and if stains are allowed time to penetrate it becomes a difficult job to take them out.

Before gloves are cleaned, they should be examined so that broken stitches and weak places can be repaired. Small holes can be button-hole-stitched and then drawn together. New buttons should be sewn on if required and existing buttons tightened. If there are button-holes, strengthen, if needed, or if press fasteners are fitted, look to the attachment.

Gloves made of finished leather such as kid, suede and calf skin should be cleaned with spirit, using petrol, gasolene, benzine or similar spirit. Begin with the cleanest of the white gloves first and place them in the spirit for a few minutes. Pick them up and rub the soiled portions with flannel soaked in the spirit.

It is a good plan to use a wooden hand as shown on the next page; they can be obtained ready made at most of the large stores, but with the measurements given, any handyman can make one from ordinary whitewood.

Wash or chamois leather gloves should be cleaned with soap and water; this method may also be used for kid gloves. Mix up a lather with soap flakes and warm water, place the gloves on the hands and rub them lightly until clean, then rinse in clean water.

As soon as a glove has been cleaned, the finger points should be drawn out and the glove stretched slightly. Leave them out in the air to dry. Delicate white gloves, especially if decorated with fancy stitchery, either plain or coloured, can be cleaned by covering them with a paste made of equal parts of Fullers Earth and powdered alum. Apply the paste thickly and brush off when dry. Finally rub them with fine oatmeal previously warmed.

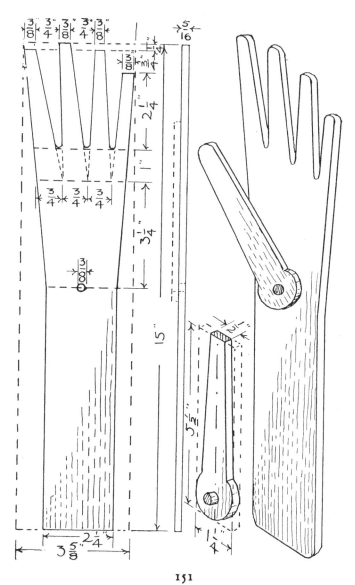

DEALING WITH THE MOTH PEST

There are few housewives who have not suffered from the ravages of the clothes moth and often with the utmost care, it is difficult to eliminate them. The adult moth, which lives about a month, is harmless, but as the moth lays about 100 eggs and each egg hatches into tiny larvae who do the damage, it is essential that preventative methods should be applied.

Apart from destroying moths whenever they are seen, all possible breeding places should be attended to. For example, cracks in the floorboards, cupboards, boxes, dark corners and in fact any place where dust can accumulate are places to be examined. Cracks can be filled with plastic wood, corners, under wardrobes, etc., should be dusted with a small brush and sprayed with carbon tetrachloride or some other suitable preparation.

If the receptacles containing clothes are kept scrupulously clean and the contents periodically shaken and aired in the sunshine, it will be difficult for the moths to breed and eggs to develop. It is a good plan to place clothing, either in moth bags, with sachets of prepared carbon inside, or in boxes wrapped up in thick paper, but in both cases it is advisable to cover joins with gummed paper tape, so that the contents are air-tight.

At least one of the drawers in a chest should be made moth proof as suggested on the next page. Obtain a piece of plywood to fit exactly inside the drawer and nail on strips of $\frac{1}{2}$ in. square wood about $\frac{5}{8}$ in. down. Thoroughly clean inside, stop up cracks and then paste on a lining of stout tar paper or brown paper. On the inside of the ledge, tack on strips of rubber draught preventer and attach turn buttons as shown; recesses should be made to allow for the thickness of the buttons.

Frequent application of the vacuum cleaner to furniture and carpets will prevent moths from finding a home. It is a good plan to take off the dust cover under spring seats and thoroughly spray with carbon tetrachloride.

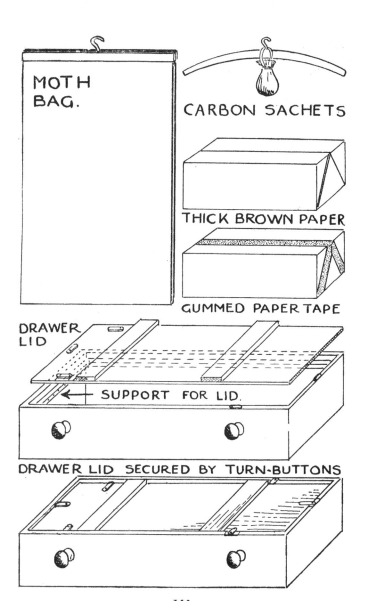

MOTH BAG.

CARBON SACHETS

THICK BROWN PAPER

GUMMED PAPER TAPE

DRAWER LID

← SUPPORT FOR LID.

DRAWER LID SECURED BY TURN-BUTTONS

TRAYS AND PARTITIONS FOR DRAWERS

It is not always convenient to completely fill a drawer, but when space is limited it is often necessary, much to the detriment of the contents. By fitting shallow moving trays or by partitioning the entire drawer, small articles can be kept together and be much more easily accessible.

Shallow trays are quite simple to make with plywood. For very little extra, the material can be obtained cut to exact size with edges planed smooth and true. With the aid of a few suitable nails and a hammer, the housewife should have no difficulty in making any number of trays.

The first thing is to decide on the size and depth of the trays. For long drawers it is better to have them running from back to front as indicated on the next page. When the drawers are narrow, trays running from side to side will do.

Having decided on the size of the trays, that is the length, width and depth, obtain sufficient pieces for the bottoms, taking care that the lengths will fit just inside the drawer. Next provide the long sides about 2 in. or so deep as required to the same length as the bottom pieces. The end pieces must be the same size as the long pieces and should be cut off to the bottom width less the thickness of two pieces of the plywood. For example, the material for a tray measuring 18 in. by 8 in., and 2 in. deep cut from $\frac{1}{4}$ in. thick plywood will be as follows :—on length 18 in. by 8 in., two lengths 18 in. by 2 in. and two lengths $7\frac{1}{2}$ in. by 2 in. The sides are nailed to the ends and then the bottom nailed to the sides. The trays rest on strips of wood, about $\frac{1}{2}$ in. by $\frac{1}{2}$ in. nailed to the inside of the drawers as indicated.

Partitions are a very simple matter. Provide pieces of plywood to fit exactly inside the drawer. Next form the grooves by nailing on strips of $\frac{1}{2}$ in. by $\frac{1}{2}$ in. wood as indicated. The materials for the strips can be obtained ready planed.

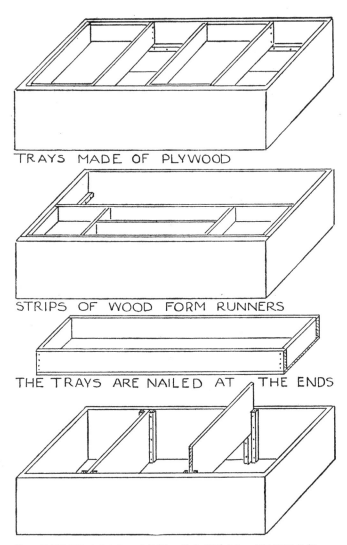

TRAYS MADE OF PLYWOOD

STRIPS OF WOOD FORM RUNNERS

THE TRAYS ARE NAILED AT THE ENDS

PARTITIONS ARE EASILY FITTED

EXTERMINATING MICE

Mice and rats are destructive vermin and are a frequent source of contagion. Efforts should be made in the first place to prevent them entering the house, but if they have established themselves, every possible means should be taken to destroy them. As a rule, mice only prove troublesome when food is available.

Preventative methods consist in filling up all holes and other places where they may find entrance. It is a simple matter for mice especially to find a way through the air bricks in the foundations of the house, and especially in houses built with cavity walls, and so gain admittance to the cavities between the ceilings and walls. Likely places where they can enter the rooms, should be filled up with plastic wood or Plasticine; neither of these substances are palatable and they form effective barriers. Large holes can be covered with tin.

The spring mouse-trap baited with cheese or fat is effective; it is also a good plan to sprinkle flour over the trap when set. After a mouse has been caught, the trap should be washed before it is used again. It will be sufficient to dip it in boiling water.

There are many kinds of poison, as well as forms of virus, specially prepared for destroying rats and mice. A useful method of using a poison is to mix equal parts of barium carbonate with dripping and stop up holes with the paste. The household cat, trained to catch mice is an excellent preventative and exterminator; if a cat is kept, all forms of poison, other than the special virus for mice, should be avoided, particularly those containing phosphorus, strychnine or arsenic. The latter should be used only if other means fail.

Food is a temptation offered to roving mice, and should always be covered up. Crumbs and scraps should not be left about. Garbage left uncovered outside the house will attract rats and mice, in fact, if they are troublesome, it is as well to burn all garbage each day.

FILL UP & COVER MOUSE-HOLES

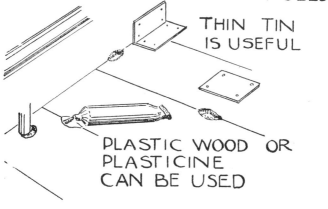

THIN TIN
IS USEFUL

PLASTIC WOOD OR
PLASTICINE
CAN BE USED

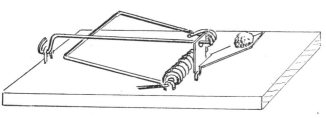

SPRING MOUSETRAPS
ARE EFFECTIVE
WHEN TASTILY
BAITED

OR

ONE OF
THESE IS
ENOUGH

HOUSEHOLD PESTS

HOUSE FLY. By far the commonest pest, the housefly, is a carrier of disease and therefore a menace to health. Generally the housefly is offered free access to all parts of the house during the summer, but it is in the kitchen particularly where they congregate. The only effective preventative is to cover with screens all doors and windows by which flies can enter, and keep them in position from early spring until late summer. It is not a difficult job to make wooden frames and cover them with muslin. If impracticable to screen all windows, at least those in the kitchen should be done.

All food in the house should be effectively covered, and waste garbage outside also be covered or burnt. Fly traps and sticky flypapers should be provided, but flies should be " swatted " as frequently as possible. Regular spraying with special preparations should be carried out, including the outside walls.

MOSQUITOES. Spraying with pungent oil such as camphor or cedar is a preventative. As mosquitoes breed in water, spray with paraffin where possible, especially wet garbage and damp corners in the garden or near the house. Where prevalent, use screens.

ANTS. Destroy nests with boiling water, place paraffin or a mixture of borax and sugar near the runs. Ants are always found in colonies and a keen look out for their dwelling places, so that they can be destroyed, will soon eradicate these pests. If very prevalent, stand tables, refrigerators and cabinets with legs in water with a film of oil on top.

BEETLES AND COCKROACHES. Keep all corners perfectly clean and free from crumbs and food scraps. Stop up all possible places of entry. Sprinkle alum or borax where they run, wash frequently with paraffin or kerosene. To exterminate pests, constant attention is needed and above all, cleanliness.

STORING FABRICS

During the winter and summer, all seasonable clothing and any other fabrics such as curtains not in use should be carefully stored in moth proof receptacles. Many housewives find the under-bed wardrobe useful for this purpose, but in addition such receptacles as cupboards, chests and boxes are often used.

The first essential in storing, either during the winter or summer, is to clean thoroughly all the articles to be stored. First remove all grease spots and dust; washable articles should be left rough-dry and clothing unless it should be washable, should be dry cleaned. White articles usually starched should be left rough-dry.

Special care should be taken with all woollen goods; even if they are placed in an air and dust proof receptacle, it is advisable to enclose them in a mothproof wrapper or bag. Ordinary brown paper can be used, but the ends and joins should be sealed with paper tape or strips of pasted paper leaving no place of entry for moths and insects. In the case of a chest or spare travelling case, the lock opening should be sealed with paper.

It is useful to prepare gummed or tie-on labels so that the contents of each packet can be readily seen. A little extra time spent in this way will save considerable trouble when it is desired to find any particular article at the beginning of the season.

Suggestions are given on page 152 to prevent the ravages of moths. Special precautions should be taken with furs, they should be stored in separate boxes lined with tar paper in preference to ordinary paper. Cedar boxes are sold for fur storage, but in all cases camphor or carbon moth balls should be enclosed before sealing up. The important thing in storage is to make quite sure that furs particularly are free from dust; thorough shaking is not always sufficient; if available a vacuum cleaner should be used. Expensive fur coats should be put in cold storage.

BUILDING DOLLS' HOUSES

Dolls' houses made from cardboard boxes generally will give as much pleasure as the most elaborately fitted house. There is an added attraction in a home-made doll's house as it can be developed room by room, decorated and furnished to individual taste.

A suggestion is given on the next page for utilising a suitable packing case. Orange boxes, fruit boxes and packing cases can be used with very little adaption, or the wood can be used to construct to a particular plan. In the design illustrated, the sides are made up with three strips, this renders the cutting out of windows a simple matter. Three strips are used for the upright partitions to allow for doors.

The dimensions of the house will depend on circumstances, a case measuring 2 ft. 6 in. long, 1 ft. 9 in. wide and 1 ft. 6 in. deep makes a roomy house and allows of furniture to be made to a scale of about 1 in. to 1 ft. Wallpapers can be home made with stick prints, or cut from an odd roll, but to conform with modern decoration, the inside of the house can be painted with poster or show-card colours.

The actual furnishing of the rooms should be carried out by the children with a little guidance. All sorts of odds and ends can be utilised, small cardboard boxes, empty matchboxes, some thin plywood and a fretsaw for the handy boy, together with some tube glue, will provide for hours of interesting work.

As far as possible the children should be encouraged to make all the furniture and fitments and only the necessary materials should be provided. The suggestions given on page 166 for paper furniture should be carried out first before anything more elaborate is attempted. Projects carried out at school can be utilised at home and, apart from a little help in difficult jobs, even the crudest attempts should be given encouragement.

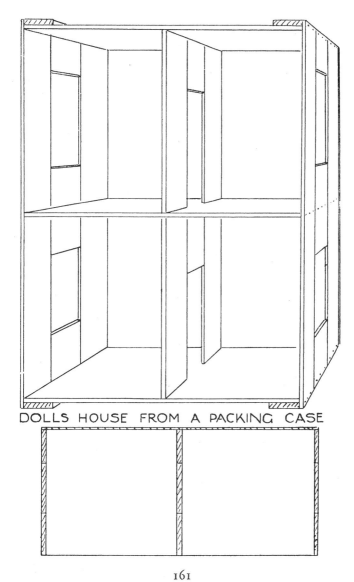

DOLLS HOUSE FROM A PACKING CASE

MODELLING FOR THE CHILDREN

Modelling in clay is a fascinating occupation for children from quite early years, and with a supply of Plasticine there are few children who will fail to become thoroughly engrossed in the manipulation of this material. It is one of the materials with which children can be left with little supervision, and they will amuse themselves for hours at a time.

Although clay modelling is taught in schools, there are many ways of using it differently at home. There are little cutters for making geometrical shapes from a flattened strip of Plasticine; these repeated and linked together with rolls will make patterns and designs of all sorts of things. Cut-out shapes of animals can be obtained, these shapes are filled in with thin layers of Plasticine and will lead the way to more ambitious work; brick and other shaped moulds into which the Plasticine can be pressed are also obtainable.

Plasticine can be obtained in 1 lb. packets and also in various outfits from a penny to a guinea. It is made in grey, red, blue, green and yellow, the possibilities for using colour make a strong appeal and provide for realistic work.

Using ordinary care, Plasticine is remarkably clean in use and has the advantage of being antiseptic. Modelling can be done on the table or on the floor, but it is advisable to provide a sufficiently large piece of American cloth on which the children can work. This material is easily cleaned and is an ideal surface for rolling or flattening the clay.

Older children who can be provided with a special playroom or have a large table in their own room should be encouraged to model farms, villages, and places of local interest. The work should be carried out by stages and as far as possible based on actual proportions worked out from approximate measurements.

FARM BUILDINGS IN PLASTICINE.

TWO PHOTOGRAPHS SHOWING USES FOR
PLASTICINE.

Photos by Harbutt's Plasticine.

163

FURNITURE IN PAPER FOR A DOLL'S HOUSE.

DOLL'S FURNITURE BY DRYAD HANDICRAFTS.

HOBBIES FOR CHILDREN

The creative instinct is so strong in children that from very early years they want to make something. The tiresome child is usually one with little or nothing to provide interest and occupation. The housewife with growing children to look after, should explore the possibilities in the large range of hobbies which are suitable for children of all ages.

Suggestions are given in these pages for building and furnishing a doll's house, for making separate rooms complete with furniture, for making odds and ends from empty matchboxes, and for the use of Plasticine in modelling.

For the younger children, there are plenty of things to be made from paper and with paper. All sorts of boxes can be utilised for making into useful articles or playing at shops, etc. Needlework is always attractive to girls, but in addition there is simple weaving, either on prepared cards or with simple looms.

For the older children, working models make a strong appeal. From small beginnings and with little expense, excellent constructional work can be carried out with meccano and other mechanical units. With a clockwork engine, a few carriages and trucks, a few yards of line, a model railway system can be developed.

Boys will appreciate a spare room, an attic or a shed in which they can do simple carpentry and make useful things for the home as well as for personal use.

It is for the benefit of children and to provide for suitable occupation during their leisure hours, that several of the " 101 " books have been written. For the little folks of ages from seven to eleven, " 101 Things for Little Folks " contains a fund of suggestions. For the girl of ten and eleven upwards, " 101 Things for Girls to Do " is full of interesting ideas, and for the boy of school age and beyond, " 101 Things for a Boy to Make," will be found of the greatest value.

DOLL'S FURNITURE IN PAPER

The illustration at the top of the next page shows how three large pieces of cardboard can be hinged together to form three sides of a room. As a substitute for a doll's house, this method of treatment is simple and effective. Windows, doors, fireplaces, wallpaper and pictures can be painted directly on the cardboard, one side being used as a living room and the other a bedroom. The cardboard should be 30 in. by 20 in.

The floor covering can be made from a piece of paper and painted with a suitable pattern to represent a carpet or linoleum. A strip of wallpaper may be used instead. Curtains can be made from pieces of muslin and can, if desired, be patterned with paint applied with a stick.

If the cardboard is 20 in. high, the proportions of the pieces of furniture should be designed accordingly. For example, the room can be considered as 10 ft. high and 2 in. will represent 1 ft. In this case the table should be 5 in. high, the sideboard 6 in. high and the small chairs 3 in. high, other measurements being in proportion.

To make the table, take a piece of stiff drawing paper or thin cardboard 18 in. by 15 in., mark off a border of 5 in., fold along the border lines, shown dotted in the diagram, and cut out legs. Paste up the corners and strengthen by angle pieces inside the corners. To make the small chairs, the paper should be 15 in. long and 9 in. wide to begin with, the back folds over at the dotted line and is pasted down.

The armchairs are made with side pieces made in the form of boxes measuring 5 in. by 5 in. by 1 in. The seat should be similarly made to 5 in. by 4 in. by 3 in., and the back 4 in. by 4 in. by $\frac{3}{4}$ in. The method of cutting out the boxes and also folding them is shown at the bottom of the page. The sideboard is also made up in box form. When pasted up and dry, the paper furniture can be painted with water colour. The fireplace shown in the illustration can be made as a shallow box.

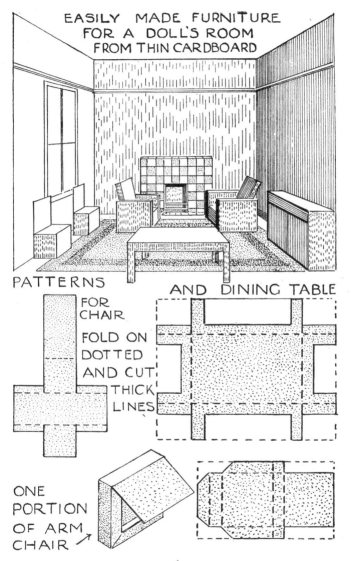

EASILY MADE FURNITURE
FOR A DOLL'S ROOM
FROM THIN CARDBOARD

PATTERNS

FOR
CHAIR

FOLD ON
DOTTED
AND CUT
THICK
LINES

AND DINING TABLE

ONE
PORTION
OF ARM
CHAIR

167

TOYS FROM MATCH-BOXES

A suggestion is given at the top of the next page for a toy locomotive and a truck made from boxes with the help of a cotton reel and a small cork or two. The engine is made from one complete box and two halves. The lower portion is formed by the outer case to make a support for the round boiler; the inner box is drawn out halfway and fixed in position with a little glue on the inside, to form the tender. The cabin and surround for the tender is made from an inner box cut in half and glued in position with gummed paper, tape or angles of paper glued on. The boiler can be made from a suitable cotton reel wrapped round with paper pasted on, or a large cork can be used. The chimney is a small cork. The wheels are slices of cork cut off with a sharp knife; they are attached with pins pushed through the side of the boxes into pieces of cork glued on inside. The wagon is made with an outer and an inner case glued together. The match-boxes should be covered with paper pasted on when complete.

The armchair is made from four boxes fixed together with glue and covered with paper. A pattern can be painted on. The dining table shown on the next page is made with two boxes and a cardboard top glued on. Poster colour is the best paint to use as it is opaque and is easily applied.

The nest of drawers illustrates a useful article easily made by children. The boxes, as many are desired, are glued together, the outside should be covered with plain paper and painted, or a patterned paper can be used. The drawer handles are made from boot buttons held in position inside with a short length of match stick. The small cabinets can be used for storing postage stamps, pen nibs, rubbers and all sorts of odds and ends; they are also useful for storing buttons, pins and needles in the workbox.

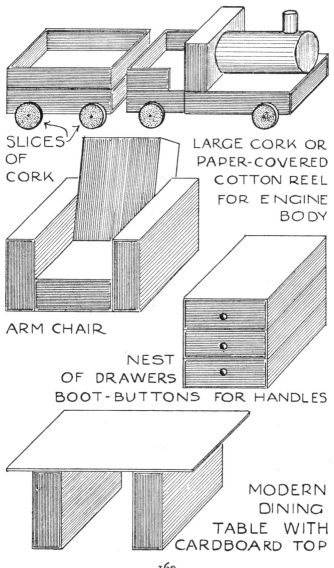

SLICES
OF
CORK

LARGE CORK OR
PAPER-COVERED
COTTON REEL
FOR ENGINE
BODY

ARM CHAIR

NEST
OF DRAWERS
BOOT-BUTTONS FOR HANDLES

MODERN
DINING
TABLE WITH
CARDBOARD TOP

FIRST AID CUPBOARD

A first aid cupboard, especially where there are children, should be considered as an essential fitment in every home. There is no need for anything elaborate.

A suggestion is given on the next page for a suitable cupboard. It will be found convenient to have two doors hinged on the sides as shown. The inner shelves should be set back to allow for projecting articles to be attached, small cup hooks should be screwed on at convenient positions to carry scissors, forceps, a spoon or two, some wooden skewers, a small magnet, etc.

The shelves should be stocked with a packet of sterilised dressings, small ones for injured fingers, medium ones for hands or feet and larger ones for other injured parts. In addition stock a packet of specially sterilised dressings for burns. Provide some suitable tin canisters to hold a supply of cotton wool, the $\frac{1}{2}$ oz. packets are convenient; also provide some plain and some sterilised lint, and some oiled silk.

Bandages of various sizes, both triangular and roller, should be provided, the latter should be in a range of widths from $\frac{3}{4}$ in. to 3 in. or so. They should be kept in a suitable receptacle free from dust.

Place on the shelves a graduated medicine glass, bottles containing iodine, sal-volatile, smelling salts, ammonia, crystals of permanganate of potash, antiseptic vaseline, one or two camel hair brushes, salicylic acid, ammoniated tincture of quinine or cinnamon and quinine, tincture of myrrh, castor oil, Famel Syrup, salt, smelling salts, crushed linseed meal, mustard, arnica and a turpentine liniment, and boracic powder. As far as possible the bottles should have glass stoppers and be different in shape. Label the bottles plainly.

Do not overcrowd the cupboard, but if there is room, bottles of eucalyptus oil and bicarbonate of soda can be added. A small dredger tin of flour is also useful for application in the case of scalds, it is better than oil.

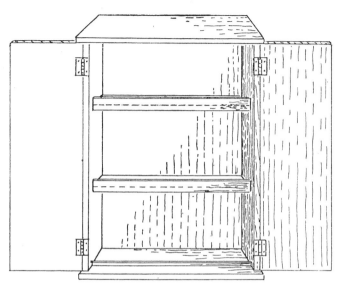

SHELVES ARE NARROW TO ALLOW ROOM FOR
SCISSORS, TWEEZERS &c. TO BE HUNG ON DOORS

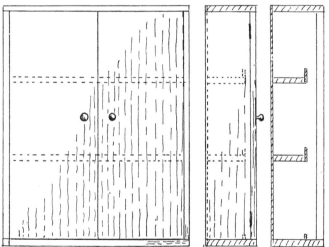

WEAVING

The art of weaving, one of the oldest of the peasant crafts, is one of the most interesting and fascinating occupations that are available for the housewife in the home. Not only can small articles be made on primitive looms, but beautiful rugs, and originally patterned and coloured fabrics offer little difficulty to those who have mastered the simple technique of weaving.

In the description of various looms on page 176 mention is made of card looms and the photograph at the top of the next page gives some illustrations, showing a few of the particularly useful articles that can be made on these simple looms. The cards are printed with the outline of the shape with dots for piercing, and in those intended for quite young children, with holes ready pierced. The materials required include a long needle and either coloured raffia, jute yarn, fine cotton yarn, twine or wool.

The lower illustration on the next page contains some more finished examples of work done on card looms, and also more advanced work done on a small table loom, similar to that shown at W 36A on page 177. It is not possible to arrange for great variety of pattern of colour in the small looms, but the possibilities are such that, using suitable yarns, most attractive work can be done with no previous experience of weaving.

It is necessary that the most suitable material is obtained, just ordinary yarns and wools can be used for any of the experimental work, but if really satisfactory work is to be done on the loom, the weaving should be done with super quality yarn spun from fine wool. As a rule, care has to be taken to provide a wool suitable for the warp ; this can be in two-ply, with three-ply for the weft. Jute, cotton and linen yarn are made specially for weaving and may be used in combination. In every case, the yarns and wools required for weaving should be purchased from a

SPECIMENS OF USEFUL ARTICLES MADE FROM
DRYAD CARD LOOMS.

MORE ADVANCED BUT QUITE SIMPLE WEAVING
DONE ON DRYAD LOOMS.

MORE EXAMPLES OF SIMPLE HAND WEAVING
ON DRYAD LOOMS.

reputable firm specialising in the requisite equipment for the craft.

It is not practicable in this book to deal with the actual process of weaving on a hand loom, the technicalities, although simple, would occupy many pages, but as it is usual for working instructions to be sent out with the looms, as there are many books on the subject, there is no need to take up space.

There are many technical terms used in weaving which should be understood before any really practical weaving can be done. The warp is the name given to the long threads first attached to the loom. It should be understood that the length of the warp must be somewhat longer than the length of material to be woven. In small looms, the separate lengths forming the warp can be joined together at the ends forming a continuous loop, but in the case of larger looms, it is necessary to attach the warp to a roller; it would be difficult to find space for it if kept in long lengths.

The weft is the name given to the cross threads; in a simple card loom, they are made with a needle, but in the larger ones, with a shuttle. The shuttle may be just a simple piece of wood or cardboard or made of wood to boat shape and fitted with rollers.

The shed is the name given to the opening between sets of the warp to allow the shuttle to run through and form the weft. There are various ways of raising the threads and it is by the variation of these methods that the main pattern is formed. The particular appliance used in looms is called the heddle, and a simple form is shown in connection with the small appliance numbered W 203 and W 36A on page 177. Two heddles are shown on the table loom illustrated on the same page; as a rule, the more elaborate the pattern, the greater the number of heddles. Generally if two-ply wool is used as the warp, either three, or four-ply should be used for the weft. A two-ply wool as a warp can be used with mercerised cotton as the weft.

LOOMS FOR WEAVING

Practical looms can be quite simple pieces of construction and range from pieces of ordinary cardboard with notched edges and pierced holes to elaborate foot power units suitable for weaving large curtains and dress lengths.

For the children, there are the simple serrated looms, made of cardboard or plywood, as illustrated at L 1. Dryad shaped serrated looms and a large variety of card looms with which such useful articles as mats, bags, egg and tea cosies, berets and slippers can be made by following the simple directions printed on the cards. The looms are used with a needle; a variety of threads can be used with them.

The Dryad board looms, shown at 35 and 35A, are inexpensive and can be used for weaving belts, ties, etc. Another practical method of weaving without a loom is illustrated at W 203. In this case the warp is made and strained between two rods, one is attached to a peg or screw hooks and the other to the waist of the weaver.

The braid and scarf loom shown at 36A, although an elementary loom, weaves a piece of material of reasonable length, quite long enough for a scarf. It is quite simple in construction and suitable for children. Simple patterns made by various arrangements of warp and weft are easily designed and carried out.

A table loom of the cottage type is shown at W 337. This is known as the " Wendicote " four-way table loom. It is ideal for the housewife and for older girls. It is fitted with side sashes for metal heddle frames, and has a swinging batten with 14 dent reed.

Table looms can be obtained suitable for weaving material up to 20 in. wide. If it is desired to go beyond this size, it is advisable to use a foot-power loom. The floor area covered by a foot-power loom varies from

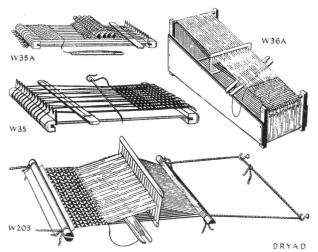

W35A

W36A

W35

W203

DRYAD

SIMPLE LOOMS FOR WEAVING BY DRYAD
HANDICRAFTS.

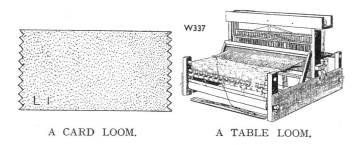

W337

A CARD LOOM.

A TABLE LOOM.

about 30 in. by 30 in. to 38 in. by 40 in.   If it is desired
to take up weaving as a practical hobby, the foot-power
loom will be found most satisfactory.   With it, such
fabrics as patterned materials, tweeds, cotton and linen
can be woven.   The difference in the time taken in
weaving on the table loom and the foot-power is considerable.

SIMPLE HOME DYEING

To be successful with home dyeing, it is essential that the article to be dyed should be perfectly clean and free from grease spots. It is not advisable to attempt at home the dyeing of non-washable fabrics, at least those of any size such as costumes, rugs, etc., preliminary dry cleaning is necessary, but small articles can be done if facilities for dry cleaning are available. Neither is it usually worth while to re-dye a previously dyed fabric unless it is chemically bleached.

The same dye will not necessarily do for all kinds of fabric. Linen and cotton will take a wool dye, but wool will not take a cotton dye. In purchasing the dye, see that it is suitable for the particular fabric, cotton, wool or silk. Cold water dyes are mainly suitable for tinting fine textured materials such as silk and muslin; boiling dyes are generally the more satisfactory for obtaining fast colours.

Considerable care should be taken in the selection of a suitable dye for coloured material. The most satisfactory colours are black and deep blue and can be used with almost any colour although blue on red is apt to produce a purple shade. White and cream articles will take any colour, but cream is not always satisfactory with either pale blue or mauve. Green fabrics can be dyed dark blue, dark red, purple and brown. Blues should be limited to dark green or dark brown. Red fabrics are difficult, but pale pink will dye almost any colour.

It is always worth while taking trouble to thoroughly cleanse the article and in the case of small made-up garments, all buttons and metal fittings should be removed and to allow for possible shrinking, the hems should be let down. This applies particularly to curtains. It should be understood that striped or spotted material, unless dyed black, will show a two-tone effect after dyeing.

Prepare the dye according to the directions given with the packet, and generally it is advisable to mix it stronger than stated. It is better to have a packet or two to spare rather than stint the quantity. For boiling, tin or zinc pans can be used; enamelled ware is liable to take some of the dye and become discoloured. Use an earthenware bowl for cold water dyes.

In mixing the dye, it is a good plan to strain it through fine muslin before it is used in case any particles are left undissolved. It is quite possible to find uneven distribution of the dye that has been caused by undissolved particles settling in portions of the fabric.

Prepare everything beforehand, not forgetting stirring rods which should be of glass if possible, but a clean length of dowel rod will do. See that sufficient dye is mixed, and remember that woollen articles will absorb a greater quantity of dye than those made of cotton or silk. Some makers state the quantity of dye required in relation to the weight of the material when dry, but it should be remembered that all articles before being placed in the dye should be wet. This applies to those dyes which combine soap and dye, and although the makers state that previous washing is not necessary, it is more satisfactory to wash the article first.

Presuming that the articles to be dyed have been washed, all grease spots removed and finally rinsed, they should be placed in the dye and lifted up and down a few times to ensure complete contact. The dye should be brought to the boil before the fabric is placed in the solution. There should always be sufficient dye in the pan to cover entirely the articles placed in it.

Usually the dye should be kept at boiling point at about five minutes and then it should be allowed to simmer for anything from fifteen minutes to three-quarters of an hour. During this time the dyeing should be watched mainly to keep the articles entirely submerged; it is for this reason that a plentiful supply of dye should be provided in the first place.

When it is considered that the dyeing is completed, it should, in the wet state, appear much deeper than actually required—the article should be lifted out of the dye pan and placed, after being allowed to dry for a minute or so, in a pan of clean cold water. Do not allow the dyed fabric to rest in the water, but rinse it thoroughly in running water and continue until no trace of the dye appears in the clean water.

Directions are usually given for adding salt or vinegar to the dye in order to set the colour. These instructions should be followed accurately, otherwise the dye may wash out to a considerable degree during the rinsing. After rinsing, the dyed articles should be left to drain; they should not be wrung out, but left to become nearly dry when they can be wrapped up in an old towel or sheet in readiness for ironing.

For the benefit of the housewife who has a loom and would like to dye the wool at home, the following instructions will be found of service. Although chemical dyes can be used, yarns dyed with vegetable dyes give much more beautiful results. First of all the fleece or yarn, handspun or machine spun, should be thoroughly scoured. Prepare the wool by taking two skeins and loosely tie them with a figure of eight tie in about four different places.

Mix up half a large packet of Lux, 6 ozs. of liquid ammonia and 2 tablespoonfuls of washing soda in about 8 gallons of water. Heat the water to about 110 degrees F. and leave the wool to soak for ten minutes, then rinse.

The next process is to soak the wool in a mordant. Alum is a convenient one mixed in the proportion of 4 ozs. to one gallon of water. Some colours require either an iron or a chrome mordant. The mordant prepares the material to take the dye and it is most important that the wool should remain in the boiling mordant solution until it has had time to penetrate thoroughly into the fibres. Rinse after mordanting and keep the wool wet until it is placed in the dye.

PURPLE. Use as a mordant, ¼ oz. of bichromate of potash in 1 gallon of water. Warm water, place the wet wool in the solution and boil for ½-hour. Use 4 oz. Cudbear mixed to a paste and place in 1 gallon of water. Enter the wool and boil for ½-hour. Take out wool, add 1 gramme stannous chloride previously dissolved in hot water, boil wool again ½-hour.

BLUE. Use alum mordant. Mix four teaspoonfuls of indigo extract with warm water, enter the wool and bring slowly to boiling point. Leave ½-hour.

GREEN. Prepare as for yellow and when dyed, place in a dye bath containing 2 teaspoonfuls of indigo extract, and simmer gently until the colour is obtained.

YELLOW. Use the alum mordant. Dissolve 2 ozs. of fustic powder in the water of the dye bath. Mix separately 1 oz. of flavin in a little hot water and add to the bath. Place the wool in the bath and boil until the desired depth of colour is reached.

ORANGE. Mix ¼ oz. cream of tartar and ½ oz. of stannous chloride with water and place in an enamelled tin not in a zinc pan. Place the wool in the solution which acts as a mordant and boil for about three-quarters of an hour. Meanwhile mix ½ oz. of flavin and 4 ozs. of madder with ¼ oz. of stannous chloride. Remove the wool from the mordant, add the flavin, madder and stannous chloride, re-enter the wool and boil ½-hour.

RED. Mix 1 oz. of cream of tartar to an alum mordant and boil for one hour. Wash once after removing from the mordant, and hang the wool in a linen bag for four or five days in a cool place and then prepare the dye by mixing 8 oz. of madder with the water. Keep the wool in the bath for one hour, but do not allow the dye to boil, keep it under the boiling point.

BLACK. Place the wool in a mordant of copperas, 2 oz. to 1 gallon of water and boil for 15 minutes. Boil 2 lb. logwood chips for ½ hour and enter the wool and boil for one hour. In all cases thoroughly rinse after removal from the dye.

DECORATIVE DYEING

Decorative dyeing is particularly interesting. There are two forms in which it can be done, one is known as Batik, the other as Tie dyeing. The former consists of covering portions of the material with wax to prevent the dye from penetrating into the fabric and with the latter, a similar result is obtained by knotting or tying the material before it is placed in the dye bath.

Batik is simple, the material is prepared by first deciding on a pattern and transferring it to the material. The hot wax can be applied with a brush, but a simple method is to use the tool used for icing sugar on a cake. The wax should be allowed to penetrate the material and allowed to dry before the fabric is immersed into the dye bath. A cold water dye should be used, as a temperature of more than 60 degrees will melt the wax. Beautiful effects are produced by the fine lines formed by the cracking of the wax. The wax can be melted out in hot water after dyeing.

Tie dyeing can be done in cold water as well as in boiling water dyes. The materials required, in addition to the fabric to be dyed are pieces of string, strips of cloth, and rubber bands. It is advisable to experiment with some cheese cloth and discover the possibilities of various methods of tieing.

A simple method is to tie the cloth in knots, say two or three at each corner of a square. Narrow lengths of material can be tied at regular or irregular intervals. The material can be rolled and tied at intervals with string or with rubber bands. Another method is to form a pattern by using buttons or flat discs and tieing the material round them. Experiments may be made by folding the material in various ways and then tying knots or binding with string. It is not possible to tell beforehand exactly how the dye will affect the material, in any case the effect cannot fail but to be pleasing, certainly original and often quaint patterns will result.

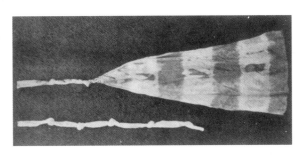

PATTERN FORMED BY KNOTS TIED AT
INTERVALS.

A PATTERN FORMED BY STRING TIED TIGHTLY
ROUND FOLDED MATERIAL.

ONE OF THE TWO THOUSAND CLASSES HELD EACH WEEK BY THE WOMEN'S LEAGUE OF HEALTH AND BEAUTY.

PRUNELLA DOUGLAS-HAMILTON, LEADER OF THE WOMEN'S LEAGUE OF HEALTH AND BEAUTY, INSTRUCTING A CLASS.

PHYSICAL CULTURE

Exercise is necessary to health; muscles not used atrophy; blood not actively circulated becomes sluggish and leads to incomplete functioning of the vital organs; a heart that ceases to beat spells death. We all know the benefits that are derived from fresh air, yet tied to our homes or business occupations during the day, they are denied to so many of us.

Mrs. Bagot Stack, who was trained at the Conn Institute, and founder of the Women's League of Health and Beauty, with twenty-five years previous experience in remedial work under the supervision of doctors, realised the need of housewives and working women and working girls for *exercise*.

With sixteen members she founded the League in 1930. To-day, nine years after its inception, the League has a membership of 175,000. In its three hundred centres in the British Isles and Dominions, over 2,000 classes are held weekly. The League believes that rhythm plays a large part in exercise, and all our classes are held to music.

I am going to give some exercises which will benefit the woman working in her home all day, but before doing so, let me remind you how desperately we need the invigoration of our bodies that only regular exercise can supply. If we are to keep entirely healthy, we must find some substitute for exercise in the open air.

Fresh air is essential. Start your day with five minutes exercise before an open window every morning. I know the average woman will say that she has little enough time as it is ! The first thing you feel on rising is the need for circulating the blood through the body. Don't think that *anyone* need have a bad circulation. It is really over-eating and over-heating; in other words, too much fuel inside the body, and too little oxygen in the lungs to maintain the balance. So open your windows, wear light, well ventilated clothes, and try the following exercises :

Exercise 1

Music. Irish Jig.
Purpose : Warmth, and to tone up the skin.
Position : Stand with feet together, hands at sides.
Exercise : (*a*) From shoulders clap all the way down the body to ankles.
    (*b*) Reverse and clap upwards. Repeat clapping down the sides from under the arms. Keep the knees straight (see figure A).

Exercise 2

Purpose : Warmth and breath control.
Position : Same as before.
Exercise : (*a*) Hop, lifting right knee to chest.
    (*b*) Same with left.
    Work (*a*) and (*b*) alternately and quickly eight times. Rest and repeat (see figure B).
Music : Irish Jig.

Exercise 3

Purpose : Warmth and breath control.
Position : Same as before.
Exercise : Same as in Exercise 2, but work to the back, kicking the pelvis with heels (see figure C).
Music : Same.

    Practise these exercises every morning, and you will find you have gained a sense of exhilaration and energy which will last you throughout the day. Not only this, but if you have flung wide your windows, you will have filled your lungs with pure, fresh air, at least *once* during the day. Breathing besides oxygenating the body is the best of all figure trainers. So many household duties mean stretching. The lungs are placed behind the ribs. If you can learn to lift your ribs right out of your waist, and to let them

expand outwards and inwards when breathing, you will soon develop that " upward buoyant poise " which is the secret of grace and which would bring less drudgery and more joy to the daily dusting, bedmaking, picture straightening, and all the dozens of things which go towards making your home beautiful.

The following breathing exercises are for slimming the bust and the waist and for giving the light upward buoyant lift of the ribs :

Exercise 4

Position : Sitting, cross-legged, ribs lifted, fingers lightly on them (see figure D).

Exercise : Breathe in quickly through the nose, drawing in abdomen. Blow out slowly through the lips, keep abdomen drawn in and allow ribs to come together without dropping downwards. Repeat four times.

Exercise 5

Position : Sitting cross-legged.

Exercise : (*a*) Close one nostril and breathe in through the other, and raise arms overhead.

(*b*) Blow out through lips, lowering arm. Twice each side (see figure E).

Exercise 6

Position : Sitting, feet straight out in front, fingers on shoulders, elbows forward.

Exercise : (*a*) Breathe in, bringing elbows out to sides at shoulder level.

(*b*) Blow out through lips and elbows forward. Repeat four times (see figure F).

Exercise 7

Position : Same as in Exercise 6.

Exercise : Same as in Exercise 6, using straight arm leverage (see figure G). Repeat four times.

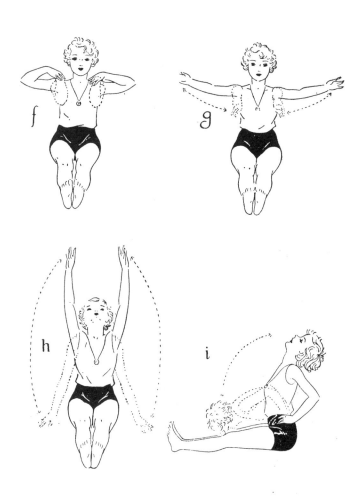

Exercise 8

Position : Sitting, arms down by sides, feet straight out in front.

Exercise : (*a*) Inhale, raising arms overhead without altering sitting position.

(*b*) Exhale, bringing arms down to the sides again (see figure H). Repeat four times.

Exercise 6

Position : Sitting, hands on hips, feet straight out in front, shoulder-blades pressed together.

Exercise : (*a*) Inhale two puffs, swaying back.

(*b*) Exhale two puffs swaying forward, being careful to keep abdomen in and shoulder-blades still pressed together (see figure I).

Repeat four times.

Practise these breathing exercises and you will find that your lungs will gain the free play they need, and that the ribs will show less tendency to collapse into the waist. You will feel taller, and gain that sense of elasticity in the waist which is so necessary to everyone, and especially to the woman who has household duties to perform.

With it all, try to keep a steady central control. While doing all your exercises aim at keeping a steady centre, *i.e.* the sacrum (lower back) down and slightly in, while keeping the abdomen up and slightly in.

The League system of exercises is concentrated *primarily* on building up control at a steady centre, namely in the abdominal region, where it trains these muscles, so essential to our health ; it can be practised day by day in our homes, while doing housework, while sitting, standing, walking—in fact everywhere and always.

CARE OF THE TEETH, HANDS AND FEET

General health depends considerably on the condition of the teeth, especially in the case of growing children. At least night and morning teeth should be cleaned with a good dentifrice, but it is preferable to clean them after every meal. Arrangements should be made with a dentist for regular and periodical attendance so that expert attention can be given to them as soon as it is necessary and this is not always evident. Equal care must be taken with dental plates, thorough cleansing is necessary to remove food from the crevices and to prevent formation of tartar which is difficult to remove.

The hands require frequent attention, especially if any of the rougher work of the household has to be done. Good rubber gloves will protect the hands from dirt and grease, but they should not be worn for long periods at a time. Cold cream, glycerine or liquid paraffin are beneficial after washing and a dusting with talcum powder will help to keep the skin smooth. In using a nail file which is preferable to scissors, hold it as indicated on the opposite page and in manicuring, have in readiness a flexible steel file, 7 in. long is a convenient size, a jug containing hot soapy water, a bowl, an orange stick, cuticle scissors, nail polish and a puff.

Neglect of the feet is likely to lead to considerable trouble. Due mainly to the need for wearing stockings and leather boots and shoes, the feet do not get the same ventilation as other parts of the body and therefore need special attention. They should be washed frequent in a warm bath containing iodine or salt and rubbed with a flesh brush. Hard skin should be prevented from forming, by using pumice stone, and corns should be treated as soon as they appear. The regular manicure of toe nails should be considered as of as much importance as those on the fingers, the same treatment being employed. An important preventative of foot trouble is massage of the muscles, especially of the toes.

CARE OF THE COMPLEXION AND HAIR

A good complexion depends on the proper functioning of the skin, and unless constant care is taken to allow the pores to perform their essential function, no amount of cosmetics will repair the damage caused by neglect.

The correct use of soap and water has an important bearing on the cleansing of the skin. Warm and not hot water and pure and not highly scented toilet soap are essentials, with a final bathe in cold water : light friction with a towel should follow.

Care must be taken in the choice of face creams. Ordinary cold cream is inexpensive and fulfils all the conditions. The most convenient method of using face cream is to apply it freely after the evening bath when the pores have been opened by bathing with warm water. Careful and thorough massage should be carried out, giving particular attention to the face muscles. It should be realised that, with age, lines will form, but the development of the lines depends mainly on habitual expression. A continually happy face will retain its pleasing contours far longer than one which shows discontent. Frequent massage will prevent the muscles sagging ; particular attention being paid to the neck and under the chin to avoid the formation of surplus fat.

Blemishes on the face may be due to choked pores or impurities in the blood. The former will develop blackheads ; these should be removed by applying a hot fomentation and then pressing the skin to expel the blemish. Acne is caused by a germ, the spot should be treated similarly to the blackhead, but the pus should be pressed out with the side of a sterilised needle and wiped with boracic lint, then touched with peroxide of hydrogen. The trouble can be prevented from spreading by using sulphur soap or ointment.

Frequent massage of the scalp is essential if the hair is to be kept healthy. Wash with a lather made of pure Castile soap or a prepared shampoo.

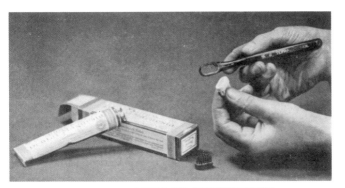

A USEFUL FORM OF TOOTHBRUSH.

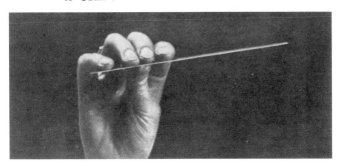

THE WAY TO HOLD A NAIL FILE.

THE ESSENTIAL APPLIANCES FOR MANICURE.

FACE MASSAGE, STARTING AT THE CHIN.

MASSAGING UNDER
THE CHEEK BONE.

PREVENTING DOUBLE
CHIN BY MASSAGE.

PRESSING OUT
BLACKHEADS.

MASSAGING THE
SCALP.

FIRST AID REMEDIES

There are many minor complaints and injuries which do not call for the services of a doctor, but in all serious cases do not fail to call in a physician immediately. It is advisable to write down the name and telephone number of the family doctor on the inside of the first-aid cupboard, and in case the usual doctor cannot be found for cases of emergency, the name of a second doctor should be included.

BILIOUS ATTACK. A suitable remedy is from 10 to 40 grains of bicarbonate of soda. Citrate of magnesia, two teaspoonfuls in a cup of water is useful for children. Usually biliousness in children is caused by incorrect diet, with a well-balanced diet containing plenty of fruit and green stuff, the trouble should not occur.

BITES of venomous and rabid animals. Wash at once with clean warm water to encourage bleeding and send for the doctor. It is an advantage to dissolve some permanganate of potash in the water used for washing, but as the treatment is surgical and not medicinal, immediate attention should be given and the wound cauterised.

BURNS. If the clothing is on fire, cover immediately with the nearest rug, overcoat, shawl, thick curtain, blanket or any such handy article. Clothing must be removed with the greatest care so that no blisters are broken, if necessary the clothing should be cut away. If any part of the clothing should adhere to the skin, remove after soaking with warm water into which some boracic powder has been sprinkled. If convenient the clothed portion may be immersed in warm water to which bicarbonate of soda has been added.

The main object in the treatment of a burn or scald is to protect the injured surfaces from the air. If nothing else is handy, ordinary flour can be sprinkled thickly on the skin, but the better plan is to use a piece of lint spread thickly with antiseptic or boracic Vaseline. On no account should a blister be pricked and do not apply oil or any ointment which does not contain a disinfectant or antiseptic; whatever is applied should be spread liberally on the dressing which should be bound up lightly.

CHOKING. In the case of small children, force open the mouth and try to hook out the obstructing body; sometimes a small spoon can be used. To deal with a small fish bone, a soft crust swallowed with water will often serve. Very little children can be held upside down; a few sudden thumps between the shoulder blades is often effective with older children and adults. If first aid remedies are not immediately effective, send for a doctor at once. An emetic can be administered to encourage vomiting.

CHAPPED HANDS. Strong soap is a frequent cause of chapped hands; wash with bran water or sprinkle boracic in warm water. The condition is often due to poor circulation and in this case calls for a tonic to improve the health. Housewives who are subject to chapped hands during the cold weather should rub the hands with pure Vaseline before beginning housework. Talcum powder is also an effective preventative.

CORNS. Innumerable remedies are available for the treatment of corns; a common and effective cure is salicylic acid. Prepared corn pads are convenient, but in the case of deep seated corns, it is advisable to employ the services of a qualified chiropodist. Hard skin on the feet should not be allowed to develop, a piece of pumice stone used after a bath is effective. Avoid tight boots and shoes and keep the feet dusted with talcum powder.

CRAMP. Cramp in the limbs can be cured by vigorous rubbing with a warm hand: press well into the muscles. Stomach cramp is usually a symptom of indigestion and can generally be relieved by applying a hot rubber bottle; a drink of hot water is often effective.

COLDS. Colds should not be treated lightly; the quickest cure is to stay in bed for a couple of days. An aperient is advisable with a hot drink following a hot bath at night. Ammoniated tincture of quinine or tincture of quinine and cinnamon are useful remedies. Usually a cold is a mild form of fever, and as a rule it is advisable to keep the patient on a light diet. Eucalyptus oil on the handkerchief is effective for a head cold, a few drops on a lump of sugar may be given occasionally. Mothers should realise that a child who develops a cold may have contracted one of the forms of contagious disease and special attention should be paid to recognisable signs.

CONTAGIOUS DISEASES. In all cases of contagious disease, however mild in form, a doctor should be consulted. Any infectious disease calls for isolation and immediate treatment. Usually a rash appears with a distinct rise in body temperature but the symptoms are not always evident at once. If a child appears feverish and is likely to have been in contact with other children, the signs should not be neglected. Such diseases as measles, mumps, scarlet fever, diphtheria and others caused by microbes may lead to serious complications if not medically attended to at the earliest possible moment.

CHILBLAINS. Children as well as adults are liable to chilblains, which are caused by poor circulation. A useful remedy is to paint the affected parts with tincture of iodine or myrrh. If the skin should be broken, apply a dressing of lint spread thickly with boracic ointment or antiseptic Vaseline. Sufferers should avoid extremes of heat or cold, wear warm clothing and take plenty of exercise.

CONSTIPATION. This trouble can be traced to incorrect diet, and can usually be cured by a diet containing wholemeal bread, plenty of cold water between meals and a generous supply of fresh fruit and green salads. Aperients will give temporary relief, such remedies as cascara, castor oil, liquid paraffin, Epsom salts and sedlitz powders are useful, but the treatment should rely mainly on a well-balanced diet and not on purging remedies.

CONVULSIONS. Occurring usually only with infants, the child should be placed in a hot bath from ten to twenty minutes. Cold water should be applied to the head. If a child is subject to convulsions, a doctor should be consulted.

COUGHS. A cough should be relieved as quickly as possible; an effective remedy is Famel Syrup. A cough is often a symptom of bronchitis, laryngitis, whooping-cough and pulmonary disease. In the case of young children it is advisable to have medical attention if a simple remedy is not effective. A cough due to a cold can be relieved by equal parts of honey and lemon juice or glycerine and lemon. The use of cough lozenges may lead to indigestion and should be given sparingly.

CUTS. Treatment for cuts is given on page 212. In all cases the cut should be thoroughly cleansed with weak antiseptic and dressed with an antiseptic dressing. Every effort should be made to remove all dirt and foreign bodies from the wound and it should be kept perfectly clean until healed.

DIARRHOEA. This is a trouble which should not be neglected. It can usually be traced to incorrect diet. A safe remedy is castor oil; the sufferer should be kept warm and given only the lightest diet until the attack is over. Diarrhoea in young children should be considered as serious, and if a dose of castor oil is not effective a doctor should be consulted.

EARACHE. Consider as serious in young children and apply a hot bran bag. A few drops of warm salad oil may be poured into the ear, but it is much safer to call in a doctor if the application of heat does not effect a cure.

EMETICS. In cases when it is advisable to give an emetic to promote vomiting, ipecacuanha wine is useful for children, the dose being one teaspoonful. For adults, a teaspoonful of salt in a tumbler of warm water is a ready remedy, or a teaspoonful of mustard made into a paste and mixed with half a tumbler of water is also effective.

EPILEPTIC FIT. Convulsive movements should not be restrained, the sufferer should lie flat and prevented from self injury, especially as regards the tongue by placing some hard substance between the teeth. In all cases a doctor should be called at once.

EYE TROUBLE. To remove any foreign matter from the eye, use a camel hair brush which should be sterilised by dipping in boiling water first and allowed to cool. If the eye is painful, apply an eye-bath with a weak solution of boracic and warm water. The upper lid can be lifted by placing a match stick over. On no account should the eye be rubbed. Styes on the eyelid can be relieved by bathing with a warm solution of boracic at frequent intervals; this troublesome but minor complaint is caused usually by a lowered state of health, and calls for a tonic or change of air.

FAINTING. Fainting is due to a diminution of the blood supply to the brain. The sufferer should be laid flat; give fresh air and apply smelling salts. A fainting fit can be prevented by sitting the person in a chair and bending the head downwards between the knees. When the attack has passed off and the patient can swallow, give a few sips of water or a few drops of sal volatile in water. Frequent fainting fits should be considered as serious and call for the attention of a doctor.

FOMENTATIONS. Hot fomentations and poultices are often required in the treatment of various complaints. A hot fomentation is prepared by using a suitable piece of lint large enough to cover the inflamed area. Place the lint on a clean face towel and roll it up, immerse the portion containing the lint in boiling water, wring the towel and lint as dry as possible, and then take out the hot lint and place it gently in position, covering it first with oiled silk and then cotton wool before bandaging. Poultices are another form of moist fomentation, crushed linseed meal and bread are generally used. The material should be made as hot as possible and should be placed in a muslin bag or a piece of muslin large enough to enclose the poultice. When a succession of poultices is needed, it is a good plan to keep one always ready in a steamer, but do not let them get too dry, as a moist poultice is more effective and keeps hot longer.

FROST BITE. On no account treat frost bite by exposing the affected part to the fire. Massage with the hands covered with coarse flannel, or woollen gloves. If caused by snow, rub with soft clean snow, and after gentle massage keep the sufferer wrapped up in a warm but not hot room.

FRACTURES. Fractures of any kind should be treated only by those having special skill in first-aid. Use the greatest care to prevent further injury, and in case it is essential to move the sufferer, the injured part should be placed in a splint to prevent any unnecessary movement to the injured part. In the case of a broken ankle, if possible remove the boot or shoe at once, if necessary slit the back seam and cut off the sock or stocking. Until the arrival of a doctor, place the sufferer in a comfortable position. A mild stimulant, such as sal volatile can be given in painful cases, but the main treatment is to prevent further movement of the injured portion until it has been set.

GAS POISONING. In cases of suffocation caused by inhaling gas fumes, place the patient in fresh air as quickly as possible, loosen the clothing and revive with smelling salts. Artificial respiration may be needed in severe cases.

HEADACHE. The cure of headache depends mainly on the cause which sometimes is obscure. Most frequently it can be traced to defective eyesight, and this should be given attention by a qualified occulist. Headaches can be caused by incorrect diet, from nervous conditions, from overheated and insufficiently ventilated rooms. Frequent recourse to such palliatives as aspirin, phenacatin, may give temporary relief, but in all cases the actual cause of the condition should be found. The commonest causes of headache apart from eye-strain are constipation, indigestible meals, strong tea and coffee, sleeping in badly ventilated bedrooms, all these are avoidable. Neurasthenic conditions, mental anxiety and worry are all conducive to headache. It should be realised that drugs have only a temporary effect and should not be treated as curative agents. The best treatment is fresh air and the avoidance of contributory causes. Headaches in children should be considered as serious if not caused by unsuitable diet ; drugs should on no account be given to children, if an aperient does not remove the trouble, a doctor should be consulted.

INDIGESTION. Generally indigestion is caused by unsuitable diet, although certain disorders of the body and nervous system may be contributory. If radical changes in the diet do not give relief medical advice should be sought. Usually a well-balanced diet, with plenty of fresh vegetables and fruit, will effect a cure. It is impossible to give a treatment which can be applied generally, so much depends on particular conditions ; it is, however, advisable to experiment with special diets until a suitable one is found. Too much starchy food is a frequent cause of dyspepsia, lack of exercise in the open air and injudicous excesses are often to blame. Even in mild cases a diet of fresh oranges for at least twenty-four hours will effect a cure, but unless this restricted diet is followed by food that will digest easily, the cure will not be permanent. Diet must be given particular attention and all food known to produce indigestion should be avoided.

INFECTION. Treatment in relation to contagious diseases has been suggested under Contagion. Much can be done to prevent infection, and all food should be protected from flies and insects liable to convey diseases. Frequent gargling will keep the throat clean, any mild antiseptic fluid can be used, but a simple and effective gargle is composed of half a teaspoonful of common salt in a tumbler of water.

INFLAMMATION. A neglected cut may cause inflammation and fester. The inflamed part should be rested and a suitable hot fomentation applied at frequent intervals. Inflammation may occur in other conditions, for example sprains. Usually hot fomentations will give relief. Unless the cause of the inflammation is evident, it is always advisable to seek medical aid.

INFLUENZA. An increasingly common complaint with often quite different symptoms, calls for considerable care in treatment. At the first signs of a feverish condition, the sufferer should be put to bed and kept warm. A mild aperient is always safe, the diet should be in liquid form, orange juice is generally beneficial. The throat should be frequently gargled, and in mild cases two tablets of aspirin will give relief. Unless care is taken in nursing even the mildest attacks, complications are likely to occur. When an influenza epidemic is prevalent, it is advisable, especially in the case of quite young children and old people, to call in a doctor. The main treatment is warmth and light diet until the feverish condition abates, when a tonic or change of air is advised.

POULTICE. Methods of making and using poultices are given under the heading of Fomentations.

POISON. In all cases of poisoning a doctor should be summoned at once. Treatment for poisoning requires special knowledge of the action of various substances. The doctor should be informed as to the probable cause ; emetics can be administered in all but corrosive poisons or those which eat away tissues such as acids or alkalis.

SICKNESS. When sickness is caused by over feeding or the presence of irritating food it should be encouraged. Sickness often occurs with children having whooping cough and is a natural condition, but if the immediate cause is not known, it may be the first symptoms of one of the childish complaints. In this case a doctor should be summoned and in the meantime the sufferer may be allowed to sip a little water.

SKIN RASH. Medical treatment is always advisable as soon as a rash develops in children. The symptom may be the forerunner of a contagious disease. Mild rashes, however, may result from irritating food; fish not quite fresh is often a contributory cause. Cases of blood poisoning exhibit a rash. Generally it can be taken that a rash calls for medical treatment.

SPLINTERS. To neglect a splinter, even if a very small one, may mean an inflamed and poisoned finger. The first-aid cupboard should contain a pair of forceps. The treatment is to bathe the area around the splinter in hot water and then pull the splinter out, first sterilising the forceps in boiling water. If it is difficult to get at the splinter, a sterilised needle should be used to enlarge the hole. After removing the splinter bathe the place with an antiseptic, and if the splinter should be dirty or poisonous, apply hot fomentations to ensure that the small wound becomes clean.

STIFF NECK. Usually caused by sitting in a draught, a stiff neck can be relieved by gentle massage with a liniment and the neck wrapped up in flannel. Warmth and rest will effect a cure.

SORES. Treat sores with antiseptic dressing and apply hot fomentations when necessary. In treating festered sores, use fomentation or poultices until the place is clean and then apply a dressing with an antiseptic ointment liberally applied. Avoid undue exposure to the air and dress frequently.

SORE THROAT. Often the first symptom of diseases especially in children, sore throats should not be neglected.

It is always safe to gargle with a mild antiseptic, but with very young children who have not learnt to gargle, they may be allowed to suck an antiseptic lozenge. Ordinary sore throat caused by dust or by a chill producing inflammation will usually give way to gargling, but when ulcerations can be seen, a gargle composed of milk of sulphur and water should be used. When children develop ulcerated throats it is probable that the tonsils require attention. In any case it is generally safer to let a doctor see the throat and prescribe the remedy.

SPRAINS. Sprains indicate that the joint has been wrenched with more or less injury to the adjacent muscles and tendons. The treatment is absolute rest, and in the case of a lower limb the legs should be kept elevated. If the sprain occurs away from home, an injured arm should be supported by a temporary sling. In the case of a sprained ankle, bind up the foot for the time being and, when home is reached, the boot or shoe should be removed.

The treatment consists of wringing out cloths in cold water, and applying them to the injured part. With severe sprains, alternate hot and cold cloths, and keep the treatment going until the inflammation subsides. The sprain should be tightly bandaged in the manner shown earlier in these pages. As a fracture is not always evident on the surface and possibly the bone may be cracked without being broken, it is always advisable to have the sprain surgically examined. Trouble may easily be caused at a later period if a sprain is neglected. Embrocations may be applied to slight sprains ; arnica is useful as well as a turpentine liniment.

STRAINED MUSCLES. For relief in the case of strained muscles, a gentle massage with liniment is a useful treatment, but the main thing is complete rest.

STINGS. The treatment for insect stings is a solution of ammonia or bicarbonate of soda. Formalin is also useful. Usually a wasp sting can be withdrawn with forceps; the ammonia should be applied with a piece of cotton wool. Scratching the place should be prevented as this action tends to drive the poison into the blood. It is worth noting that a weak solution of Epsom salts or some eucalyptus oil will keep off insects.

SUNSTROKE. The sufferer should be removed to a cool place, all tight clothing loosened and provide plenty of fresh air. Cold water may be sponged on the head and neck. Avoid stimulants and give only cold water to drink.

TOOTHACHE. As a temporary relief, the gums may be rubbed with tincture of myrrh or oil of cloves. The correct treatment is a dentist. It is a mistake to apply warmth outside the face in case there is an abscess at the root of the tooth; generally this treatment will only aggravate the trouble.

WARTS. There are many kinds of warts, and it is advisable to let a doctor give them the necessary attention.

WHITLOW. A whitlow is generally caused by a neglected scratch or splinter. Relieve by dipping the finger in hot water or use a poultice. Actually there is a small abscess, and as soon as it bursts treat as for a sore and keep the place clean.

FIRST AID BANDAGING

For first aid bandaging, the triangular bandage has a number of uses, it can be used as a sling or for rapid bandaging of splints when necessary. The complete bandage is shown at A in the top left-hand corner of the next page, the right angle at the top is called the Apex, the lower corners are the Ends, and the bottom is called the Base. The distance from the Apex to the Ends should measure from 38 in. to 42 in.

The first fold is shown at B, and consists of placing the Apex on a line with the base. In the second fold, as indicated at C, the upper edge at B is folded over to the base again. This is known as the broad-fold. To form a narrow-fold, bring the upper edge down to the base again.

The ends of a triangular bandage should always be tied with the reef knot, as illustrated in stages on the next page. It will be seen that after tying as at A, one end is folded back along itself as at B. The next stage consists of crossing the end at right angles, as at C, pull the tip through the loop as at D and E, and then pull tight as at F.

Two methods of using the triangular bandage are illustrated. In one case the whole of the open bandage is utilised, the two ends are tied together with the reef knot, the Apex being pinned over when used as a large sling for the arm. The triangular bandage when folded to either a broad- or a narrow-fold can be used as a narrow sling as shown at the bottom of the next page. As a rule the large arm sling should be used for all fractures and injuries to the hand and fore arm. The small arm sling is used for all cases of fracture to the upper arm; it will be seen in the diagram on the next page that a small arm sling would give little support to an injured forearm. For further information on first aid bandaging, consult " First-Aid Bandaging," by William E. Bradford, published at 1s. 6d.

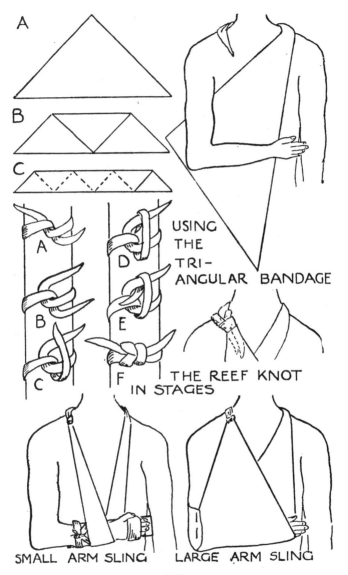

A

B

C

A

B

C

D

E

F

USING THE TRI- ANGULAR BANDAGE

THE REEF KNOT IN STAGES

SMALL ARM SLING

LARGE ARM SLING

USING ROLLER BANDAGES

Roller bandages are available in widths from 1 in. to 6 in., the most convenient sizes for general use being 1 in., 2 in. and 3 in. Cotton and linen bandages are used for fixing dressings, calico for binding splints, and flannel and crepe for painful joints.

The illustrations on the next page show the stages in bandaging the thumb and finger. In dealing with the thumb, begin with a turn or two round the wrist, leaving a few inches free. Bring the bandage as far down the thumb as it is necessary to bandage and give a complete turn as at A. Carry the bandage over the back of the hand, give a turn round the wrist and back over the thumb, as indicated at B. Continue, as shown at C, until the thumb is covered with the bandage well up to the wrist and finish off by tying to the free end or fasten with a safety pin.

In dealing with a finger bandage, begin with a turn or two round the wrist and then carry the bandage down to the particular finger to be bandaged. To fix a dressing below the first joint, the bandage can be carried over the finger as indicated at A. Wrap the bandage round the finger so that the rounds overlap about half-way, and then tie to the free end.

In the case of injury to the top of the finger, the bandage should be carried to the finger tip, given a double fold and then wrapped round the finger, as at B, and continued as at C, when the two ends are tied with a reef knot or fastened with a safety pin.

In using a bandage always begin on the inside and unroll the bandage outwards. No more than a turn at a time should be done, so that only a small amount of the bandage is unrolled at one time. Generally the bandage is bound spirally or in a figure of eight fashion. As a rule soiled bandages should be thrown away after use, but bandages made of calico, flannel or crepe can be washed and rewound ready for use.

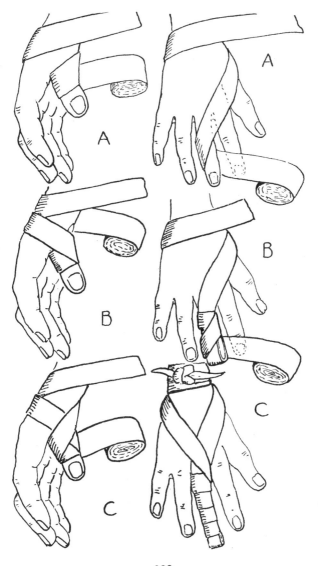

209

ANKLE, ARM AND KNEE BANDAGES

Sprained ankles require careful bandaging, a 2 in. wide bandage usually being sufficient. As a rule it is advisable to begin the bandaging near the toes and continue well up the calf of the leg in order to provide as much support as possible to the muscles.

The first stage, as illustrated on the next page, consists in wrapping a length of bandage round the upper part of the ankle, leaving at least 6 in. free. Carry the bandage down to the little toe and round the foot under the ball of the big toe. Continue round again and carry the bandage behind the heel just below the ankle bone, leaving quite half the width projecting beyond the heel. Actually the bandage should just catch the back of the heel as indicated at A.

Continue the bandaging over the instep, behind the foot as shown at B and gradually work under the heel to well above the ankle as indicated at C when the ends can be fastened together with a safety pin or tied with a reef knot. As the portion of the bandage under the heel is covered over, fold it in to leave a smooth surface.

The elbow and knee are bandaged similarly. Beginning with a turn or two above the point of the elbow which should be flexed. The next turn should be below the point as shown at A, the bandage covering the lower third of the first turn. Continue round and carry the bandage above the point again so that the upper third of the first turn is covered. Continue in this way, first on one side of the point and then on the other until sufficient of the elbow has been bandaged, when it is finished off above the elbow as shown at B.

In dealing with a knee bandage, allow plenty of room on each side of the knee cap and keep the knee flexed during the binding. The bandaging should be finished off above the knee with two turns before the ends are pinned or tied together; it is usual to finish with a safety pin rather than with a reef knot.

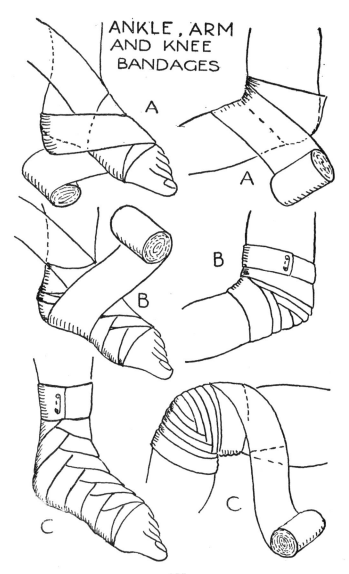

ANKLE, ARM
AND KNEE
BANDAGES

A

A

B

B

C

C

METHODS OF STOPPING BLEEDING

Excessive bleeding should be stopped as soon as possible, and in the case of deep cuts or other injuries it is advisable to send for a doctor at once. Cuts on the hand should be washed immediately, preferably with an antiseptic solution; a few crystals of permanganate of potash dropped into the water will do. Cover the cut with a sterilised dressing, and use a roller bandage as required. Small cuts and scratches may be treated with iodine, but in all cases it is advisable to wash the injury thoroughly first, and cover with a suitable bandage to prevent dust or dirt entering.

In the case of deep hand cuts, one method is to cover the wound with antiseptic dressing and grasp a tennis or hard rubber ball firmly as shown on the next page. If the wound is in such a position that pressure cannot be conveniently applied, bind the arm just below the wrist, if necessary twisting the knot with a wooden skewer to tighten it. The bandage should be kept in position until the bleeding stops or until the doctor arrives.

In dealing with bleeding from the nose, it is not always advisable to stop the bleeding at once. In the case of old people, bleeding at the nose is often salutary, as it prevents congestion. The patient should be seated with the head well back and when possible with the arms upraised. A cold wet sponge can be applied to the back of the neck; if ice is available it will be found beneficial. As a rule it is not advisable to continually remove bloodclots; allowed to remain they will gradually prevent the bleeding and keep the air and impurities from the vein.

In all cases of hæmorrhage, the patient should be kept as quiet as possible, exertion of any kind should be avoided until all signs of bleeding have disappeared. Cases of internal hæmorrhage, apart from the nose, should have the immediate attention of a doctor.

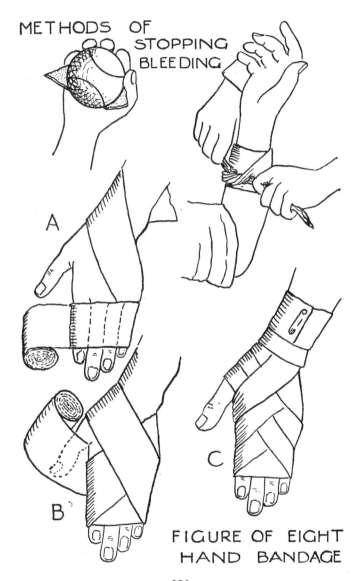

METHODS OF STOPPING BLEEDING

A

B

C

FIGURE OF EIGHT HAND BANDAGE

213

INDEX

Ants, 158

Balance, Spring, 83
Bandages, Ankle, Arm and Knee, 210
—— Using Roller, 208
Bandaging, First Aid, 206
Baskets, Bulb, 58
—— Wastepaper, 86
Bedroom, Furnishing, 9
Bedstead, Modernising, 70
Beetles, 158
Bilious Attack, 195
Bites, 195
Blankets, Washing, 148
Bleeding, Stopping, 212
Bowls, Bulbs in, 57
Boxes, upholstered, 88
—— Window, 60
Brillo, 102
Brocade, 23
Brushes, Care of, 53
Burns, 195

Cane, Reseating in, 50
Carpets, Cleaning, 144
—— Repairing 138
—— Sweeping, 37
Chapped Hands, 196
Chilblains, 197
Children, Hobbies, 165
—— Modelling for, 162
—— Toys for, 168
Chintz, 23
Choking, 196
Cleaning, Dry, 149
Cockroaches, 158
Colds, 197
Colour Schemes, 4
Coloured Materials, Washing, 148
Complexion, 192
Constipation, 197
Contagious Diseases, 197
Covers, Loose, 20
Convulsions, 198
Corns, 196
Cramp, 196
Crockery Repairs, 106
Culture, Physical, 185
Cupboard, First Aid, 170
Curtains, 16, 17, 18, 19
—— Hooks and Rails, 26
Curtains & Valances, 28
Cushions, Making, 94
Cuts, 198

Damask, Satin, 24
Darning, 100
Day Nursery, 12

Decoration, Flower, 33
—— Furnishing, 13
Diarrhoea, 198
Distempering, 126
Doll's House, 160
Doll's Furniture, 166
Doors, Easing, 130
Drawers, Easing, 130
—— partitions, 154
Duties, Household, 1
Dyeing, Decorative, 182
—— Simple Home, 178

Earache, 198
Electric Cords, 74
—— Irons and Ironing, 143
Elizabethan Fabrics, 16
Emetics, 198
Enamel, Using, 134
Epileptic Fits, 199
Eye Trouble, 199

Fabrics, 22
—— Storing, 159
—— Washing, 146
Fainting, 199
Faucets, Washer, 72
Feet, Care of, 191
Fireplaces, 108
First Aid Cupboard, 170
—— Remedies, 195
Flex, Mending, 74
Floors, Staining, 120, 122
Flower Decoration, 44
Fomentations, 199
Fly, House, 158
Fractures, 200
French Polishing, 132
Frost Bite, 200
Fuse, Renewing, 76
Furnishing, Bedroom, 9
—— Day Nursery, 12
—— Decorative, 15
—— Period, 16
Furniture, Paper, 166
—— Selecting, 6

Gardening, Window, 60
Gardens, Table, 54
Gas Burners, 140
—— Poisoning, 200
—— Stove, 140
Georgian Fabrics, 16
Gloves, Cleaning, 150
Gulleys, Cleaning, 116

Hair, Care of, 192
Handles, Loose, 114
Hands, Care of, 191
Hat Wardrobe, 84
Headache, 200
Hobbies, Children, 165
—— Housewifes, 52

Hooks, Rails, and Curtain, 26

Indigestion, 201
Infection, 201
Inflammation, 202
Influenza, 202
Irons and Ironing, 142

Jacobean Fabrics, 16

Knee Bandages, 210
Knitted Garments, Washing, 148
Knife Handles, 114
Knives and Scissors, Sharpening, 112

Lamp Shades, 42
League of Health and Beauty, 185
Linen, Darning, 100
—— Marking, 98
Linoleum, 136
Looms Weaving, 176
Loose Covers, 20

Marie Antoinette Curtains, 29
Measures & Weights, 82
Menus, Arranging the, 2
Meters, Reading, 78
Mice, 156
Mildew, 119
Modelling for Children, 162
Mosquitoes, 158
Moth Bag, 153
Moth Pest, 152
Muscles, Strained, 204

Needle Weaving, 31

Paint, Using, 134
Paintwork, 128
Pans and Pots, 103
—— Mending, 104
Pantry, Shelves, 62
Paper Furniture, 166
Pelmet Styles, 38
Pelmets, Supports, 40
Pests, 152, 158
Physical Culture, 185
Plasticine 162
Poisons, 202
Pots and Pans, 103
—— Mending, 104
Pouffes, Making, 96
Poultice, 202

Refrigerators, 64

Satin, Damask, 24
Scales, Household, 82
Scissors, 112
Seagrass, Seating, 47
Seat, Window, 68

Sewing Machine, 90
—— Attachments, 93
Shellac Polishing, 132
Shelves, Pantry, 62
—— Kitchen, 67
Shoe Tidy, 84
Sickness, 203
Silks, Washing, 148
Sink, Stopped up, 116
Skin Rash, 203
Sores, 203
Sore Throat, 203
Sprains, 204
Splinters, 203
Stains, Removing, 118
Stiff Neck, 203
Stings, 204
Stitches, Decorative, 32
Stow-a-way Kitchen Laundry, 35
Strained Muscles, 204
Sunstroke, 205

Table Gardens, 54
Table Linen, 100
—— Marking, 98
Tap, Washer, 72
Tapestry, 24
Teeth, Care of, 191
Thermometers, 80
Thor Stow-a-way Laundry, 34
Throat, Sore, 203
Tidy, Shoe, 84
Tie Dyeing, 182
Tiles, Fixing, 108
Toothache, 205
Toys from Match-boxes, 168
Trays for Drawers, 154
Tudor Fabrics, 16

Upholstered Boxes, 88

Valances, 28
Victorian Fabrics, 18

Wallpaper, Cleaning and Repairing, 125
Walls, Distempered, Cleaning, 126
Wardrobe, Hat, 84
Warts, 205
Washer, Fitting, 72
Washing and Ironing by Electricity, 34
Weaving, 172
—— Looms for, 176
—— Needle, 31
Weights & Measures, 82
Whitlow, 205
Window Boxes, 60
—— Gardening, 60
—— Seat, 68
Windows, Easing,
Woollens, Washing,

214